# THE DELIVERER

## & THE TEN COMMANDMENTS

# THE DELIVERER

## & THE TEN COMMANDMENTS

Written by DANIEL JOSEPH OWEN
Illustrated by SARAH GLORIA TONEA

*The Deliverer & the Ten Commandments* by Daniel Owen

*Copyright*: © 2025 Daniel Owen

First printing, 2025.

ISBN: 979-8-218-89143-5 (Softcover)

First Edition: December 2025

Cover Design by Daniel Owen

Illustrations copyright: © 2025 Daniel Owen

Illustrator: Sarah Tonea

This book is a work of non-fiction that seeks to explore the historical and cultural context of the Ten Commandments from an Ancient Israelite perspective. The individuals mentioned are real historical and biblical figures. While the author has made every effort to ensure historical accuracy and fidelity to relevant biblical texts and scholarship, the interpretations and explanations offered are those of the author and do not necessarily reflect the official doctrines or beliefs of any specific religious denomination, group, or organization. Readers are encouraged to use discernment and consult a variety of sources for their own spiritual understanding and education. This book is intended for informational and educational purposes only.

**Miqlat Press** (*a division of the Michael S Heiser Foundation*)
2026 The Woods Dr, Jacksonville, FL 32246

www.michaelsheiserfoundation.org

*For Havah, Eliyah, Moriyah & Shayah*

*"More than the Stars,*
*Higher than the Mountains*
*& Deeper than the Sea."*

# Acknowledgments

To my wife, Teodora—I am eternally grateful that Yehovah was so kind and generous in bringing us together. Your endless curiosity, thoughtful feedback, encouragement and patience made this endeavor possible. Not one page would exist without you. Te iubesc, draga mea.

To my children—you are the reason I wrote this book. May your lives be ever filled with wonder and awe at the splendor and goodness of our Creator. Your curiosity and questions, not to mention the character you are all developing, make me so very proud to be your Papa. I love you.

To the rest of my family and friends—thank you all for encouraging me to take this gigantic leap outside of my comfort zone, for your prayers, and for offering an ear when I needed to work through an idea.

To Brent—my brother, our challenging discussions are a constant source of inspiration. Thank you for being an ear to ideas, an example for so many, and for helping me deconstruct my own lenses.

To Pastor Rick Struckel—all of this is your fault. You gave me a place to ask unfiltered questions when my life was teetering toward chaos. Had Yehovah not been so gracious in bringing me to your doorstep, I can't imagine where I'd be today. Thank you for your endless wisdom, guidance, encouragement and—the most valuable gift of all—your time. I will pay it forward.

To Drenna Heiser-Hollander—thank you for the opportunity of a lifetime, and for trusting me to write this book. Mike inspired so many, and I, for one, look forward to the day I can thank him face to face.

Finally, to every parent and child who opens this book—I hope you find something in these pages that stays with you for a lifetime. And, as I pray for my own family each day, I pray that Yehovah watch over each of you and cause you to flourish. May he be your refuge and shine over you with his favor. May he give you his loving attention, and cause you to lack no good thing. In the name above all others—Yeshua the Messiah—Amen.

# A Note to Parents

As a piece of literature, the Bible has some very raw, human themes—some of which may not be suitable for all ages. As such, this book is intended to be read by parents and children together, allowing you to decide what is appropriate for your child. My hope is that this book helps families on their journey learn more about *Yehovah*, specifically, who he is and what he expects of each of us. Along the way, we will explore challenging ideas, some of which may be new. Yet, the purpose of this book isn't to debate theology or be controversial. Rather, it is to provide practical understanding for daily life.

Whether we are young or old, children or parents, life is about both learning and growing as *imagers* of the Creator. As such, it's not *what* we know, but what we do with that knowledge that matters most. You will find many references to Bible verses in the following pages. A complete list is found on page 37. You will also see words written in red, each of which is defined in a glossary that begins on page 31. I cannot recommend enough that you stop and read each reference and glossary entry as you encounter them. On the following pages, we will explore some ideas that will set the stage for the understanding the Ten Commandments.

## Deconstructing Our Lenses

As the message of the *Messiah* spread outward from Judea, the number of non-Jewish followers of *Yeshua* rapidly increased, eventually overtaking the total number of Jewish followers. Many of these non-Jewish men and women came to follow Yeshua after having been raised within worldviews that were heavily influenced by paganism and the philosophies of Ancient Greece.

Why does this matter? The lenses we use to see the world can influence how we understand the Bible. And although it is not universal to all Greek philosophy, the prioritization of one's beliefs over their actions is certainly rooted in Greek philosophical propositions, such as Plato's *Ladder of Love*, a view embedded in the rationalism of Hellenistic culture. Similarly, Aristotelianism valued contemplation as the highest good, while Epicureanism sought mental tranquility through understanding. Neoplatonism intensified this by prioritizing one's mental ascent over their practical behavior. Meanwhile, early Christian Gnostic sects greatly emphasized esoteric knowledge, as opposed to the more balanced position regarding faith and action held in some Orthodox traditions.

In fact, Augustine integrated Platonism, stressing salvation through one's belief and grace in *Confessions*, influencing Scholasticism's focus on doctrinal clarity. The Council of Nicaea codified the power of creeds, while Descartes proposed the famous line, "I think, therefore I am." In *Sola Fide*, Martin Luther, though rightly opposing the Catholic Church's practice of buying atonement through indulgences, has often been misunderstood as arguing that faith comes through one's beliefs rather than active, trusting loyalty. By the time of the Enlightenment, the focus was largely on individualism and personal ideology as being central to one's morality. Understanding was often equated with an elevation of the soul closer to the divine. These morally deceptive philosophies infiltrated faithful congregations around the world with an undeniable and lasting influence. Yet, as elegant as they may sound, they are inaccurate reflections of an Ancient Israelite worldview wherein one's beliefs were only as meaningful as the practical morality that they required.

In other words, many in the Greek world viewed the concept of *righteousness* with a different lens than that which is found in the *Tanakh*—or Old Testament, wherein righteousness is not a state of enlightenment or intellectual alignment with a particular *truth*. Rather, biblical righteousness is one's good standing in the eyes of the Creator. In other words, righteousness is determined by one's *loyalty* to Yehovah, which is expressed through their *obedience* to his established moral standard. Thus, a biblical worldview places less value on one's ideology alone, and more on their conduct. **(See James 2:14-25.)**

Despite this being the reality, within the expanding Christian world, righteousness and enlightenment became more and more synonymous. Repeated calls by the apostles for brotherly love and *reconciliation* in the *New Testament* were set aside as theological lines were drawn between believers based upon their preferred worldviews, with these divisions quickly spreading around the globe.

I am proposing that perhaps God cares less about our ideological beliefs than he does about what we do with them. **(See Matthew 25:31-46.)** The God of Israel doesn't lose sleep over, let's say, the stance we hold on generosity toward the poor. He is, however, quite concerned whether or not we are, in fact, generous. **(See 1 Timothy 6:17-18; James 2:15-16; 1 John 3:17-18; Matthew 25:31-46; Proverbs 19:17; Proverbs 21:13; Acts 10:1-4; Isaiah 58:6-10.)** That's not to say God only cares about what we do, as he's certainly interested in the intention and sincerity with which we do it. **(See 1 Corinthians 13.)** In the end, I think it's worth reiterating that righteousness in the eyes of God is not about creeds or belief systems that merely take up space in our minds. As we journey through the Ten Commandments together, my hope is that we will begin to see with fresh eyes what the Creator of the Universe expects of his children. **(See James 4:17.)**

**Grace, Faith—or both?**

There is certainly a moral imperative to follow God's ways. Yet, by definition, Yehovah's *mercy* is completely unmerited. In other words, *redemption* isn't something that we can earn—ever. On the contrary, obeying God's

*Commandments* was not ever a means by which one could earn *salvation*. Instead, it was the defining trait of those who had been redeemed. The *Children of God* were commanded to abandon their former *wickedness* and *rebellion* and *turn* to God and his ways, and, by doing so, demonstrate their *loyal obedience* by placing their trust in the One who had redeemed them, rather than each doing what was right in their own eyes. **(See Deuteronomy 12:8; Ezekiel 18:21-32.)**

Imagine you were convicted of a terrible crime—let's say murder. You were found guilty and awaiting sentencing. You were instructed to drive to the courthouse in order to be sentenced, and handed over to the state. Do you think that by keeping all the traffic laws on your way to the courthouse the judge would be justified in absolving you of your crime of murder? Obviously not! Yet, when you arrived at the courthouse you were told that the punishment of execution that was due had been paid in full—you were free to go. How would you feel toward the one who took your punishment? And having been set free, would you walk out of that courthouse and start breaking the law? Likewise, breaking God's commandments means we are guilty. Keeping them certainly does not absolve us. Yet, having been forgiven, keeping God's commandments is a sign that we have been redeemed and keeps us in good standing with the Creator.

Still, for some there may be confusion about how non-Jewish followers of Yeshua ought to live in regards to the *Torah* commandments. Aren't they just for the Jews? Why should non-Jewish followers of the Messiah keep them? As is often the case, it helps when we define a few words so that we can begin on the same page.

### Defining Terms

You may or may not have learned that Torah is the Hebrew name for the first five books of the Bible. The word is typically translated as "*Law*" in English, since the books establish the moral and civil code of Israel following their exodus out of Egypt. However, that term is a legal term that sounds sterile and harsh to modern ears. The word Torah really means "teaching, guidance and instruction," and is better understood as the instructions for life, like those given by a parent to their child. Yes, the Torah certainly contains commandments, or laws, but as a whole it is the practical guidance from the Creator to his people so they can live at *peace* with one another and with him.

In addition to Torah, two common words that we often hear in Christianity are *good* and *evil*, but defining them may be more difficult than you think. Try it yourself. Take a moment and try to clearly and concretely define those two words. It's not as easy as you might think, is it? In Hebrew, the word for "good" is *tov* and the word for "evil" is *ra'a'*. The easiest way to remember their definitions is to imagine that Yehovah made everything for a specific purpose. In other words, as long as created things function exactly as they were intended, they are tov, or functional. If, however, they are dysfunctional, or work in a way the Creator did not intend them to, they are ra'a'. For example, a fig tree is supposed to bear figs in the right season. If it does, it is a good tree. If not, it is not a good tree. Trees that produce fruit get pruned. Trees that don't produce get cut down and burned. **(See Matthew 7:15-20.)**

*Sin* is another word we often hear, but few may understand what it really means in a practical sense. In Hebrew, the verb *chata* means "to miss," as in "to go astray." In essence, the word means "to miss the mark." In this way, sin can be understood in practical terms as doing something in a way that God did not intend, design or allow, thus straying beyond the boundary that the Creator established. These boundaries exist to protect us, but we will explore that later.

On the other hand, Torah is Yehovah's teaching, guidance and instruction that shows us how things are to function properly, exactly as the Creator intended. As long as we follow the Creator's instructions, we won't stray. In fact, the word Torah comes from the word *yarah*, which means "to teach," as well as "to shoot," as in an arrow. In essence, God's Torah teaches us how to hit the mark, or live a life as God intended.

## The Boy & The Road

I am a visual learner, so I often tell parables when I teach Bible studies. One of my favorites goes something like this: Imagine a father teaches his son not to walk into the road near their home because it's dangerous. The father explains that the road is no place for a boy to play, and walking into it may hurt him, or worse. After teaching his son the lesson about the dangers of the road, the father kisses the boy on the forehead and goes inside to work on the house. A few moments later, the father looks out from a window to check on his son and, to his horror, he sees the boy playing in the street.

What does the father do? Does he run outside and kill his son for entering the road? Of course not! That would be insane—evil, in fact. The father does not harm his son. First, he shouts for him to come back. If the son does not hear, the father runs into the road, pulling his son out of danger—even if that means taking a fatal hit himself to protect the boy. The father is not dangerous; the road is. In the very same way, Yehovah's commandments exist to protect us, just like that father's instructions, from things that would harm or destroy us. Yehovah is not sitting atop a cloud waiting for you to make a mistake so that he can strike you down. He is your Maker—your loving Father—and he gave us the Torah for our protection. **(See Deuteronomy 30:15-20.)** In fact, **Psalm 19:7** tells us, "*The Torah of Yehovah is completely perfect, turning the soul* (as in from sin to righteousness.)" Maybe this all feels like a foreign idea. Let's dig a little deeper.

## Under the Law?

Neither the Old nor New Testaments portray keeping the Torah as being the means through which mankind can be forgiven for sin. Even in the Torah, redemption has always been an act of the Creator's mercy toward us, while the role of God's teaching has always been that of a guide—his divine standard for righteousness. **(See Ephesians 2:8-10; Deuteronomy 30:15-16.)** So, the Torah defines moral behavior. It doesn't have the capacity to redeem wickedness and rebellion; it just shines a light on it—that's its job. In fact, keeping the Torah never even redeemed the Israelites!

I always ask my Bible students this question: "Which came first, Yehovah's merciful redemption of Israel out of slavery in Egypt, or the giving of the Torah at Mount Sinai?" The story clearly tells us that the commandments only came after the people were already redeemed, an event that required the blood of a perfect lamb on *Pesach*! The blood of the perfect lamb marked those who belonged to Yehovah, so when he came to destroy wickedness they would be protected from death. Sound familiar? It should! **(See Exodus 12:13; Isaiah 53:7; John 1:29; Matthew 26:28; 1 Peter 1:19; 1 Corinthians 5:7; Ephesians 1:7; Hebrews 9:14; 1 John 1:7; Revelation 1:5; Revelation 5:6; Revelation 7:9; Revelation 21:27.)**

Within the Torah there existed a set of procedures for *atonement* via a complex system of animal sacrifices. This was temporary and fully replaced once and for all with the atoning sacrifice of the Messiah, whose death paid for the debt of sin for all who belong to him. **(See Hebrews 7:11-28; Hebrews 9:11-28; Hebrews 10:1-31.)** In the above verses, note the distinction between "law," as in God's perfect and eternal moral instructions, and "law," as in the former sacrificial system, which has been replaced by the Messiah's atoning sacrifice. **(See Matthew 5:17-19; 1 John 5:2-3.)** The same English word is used for two distinct ideas, often causing readers confusion.

So, while keeping Torah can never earn salvation, Yehovah's redeemed children are supposed to keep the commandments, bearing the fruit of salvation. **(See 1 Corinthians 7:17-19.)** Since we have already rebelled against God's commands, we face justice. Keeping the commandments after the fact will not be sufficient to atone for our former wicked deeds. Instead, it is the blood of the Messiah alone that reconciles us back to God, freeing us from the curse of death. Yet, Paul emphasizes that our trust in Yeshua does not mean that we reject the Torah. Instead, we are to uphold it! **(See Romans 3:21-31; 1 Corinthians 7:19.)**

Therefore, the sacrificial system, which Yehovah never desired to begin with, has been abolished forever. **(See Hosea 6:6; Isaiah 1:11–17; Micah 6:6–8; Psalm 40:6–8.)** However, the Creator still requires his people to do what is right. The standard for what is right is found in the Torah and the New Testament's explication of it. It is forever the moral standard of God as affirmed by the Messiah, whose teachings pointed out humanity's tendency toward rebellion, self-righteousness, pride, preference for traditions, and empty legalistic observances. Instead, New Testament authors called upon God's people to be the embodiment of God's moral standard.

In fact, in **1 John 3:4**, "sin" is explicitly defined as "*lawlessness*," or anomia in Greek, wherein the word literally means "no law," or more specifically, "no Torah." The writer reinforces the metric with which we must identify transgression in order to guide our moral conduct.

Remember our example of the murderer who was forgiven. No amount of good driving could remove the guilt for the blood on his hands. Yet, through forgiveness he realized that his way of doing things had nearly destroyed him. He surely wants to turn his life around, but where does he find a better way? Similarly, we who follow Yeshua have died to sin and are exhorted to present ourselves to God as instruments of righteousness, living under the grace of God rather than continuing in our former ways that nearly led to our destruction. **(See Romans 6:15-18.)** Yet, some may argue that grace has licensed the abolition of the Torah, or what they call *Law*. Yet, it was not the Torah of Yehovah that was done away with, but God saw it fit to make a new covenant, one in which he would write his Torah on our hearts! **(See Jeremiah 31:31-34.)** And if not found within God's moral instructions for humanity, where on earth do we find a better way to live? The New Testament writers call on us to live out a transformed life that honors the Messiah's sacrifice by upholding God's moral standard.

Something far greater than the former covenant has surely come! In this new covenant, non-Jews like myself have been invited to join Yehovah's family, and the former need for animal sacrifices has been fully accomplished in the death of the Messiah. So, if we rightly desire to be faithful to our Redeemer, we must reject lawlessness and walk in loyalty to the Creator. And we can take comfort knowing the Messiah promises to make his home within us, filling us with the very Spirit of Yehovah so that we might be empowered to never again turn away from his ways. **(See John 14:15-24; Ezekiel 36:27.)**

My prayer is that through this book you might gain wisdom and understanding to see just how gravely we need the promise found in **Jeremiah 31** and delivered in **Acts 2**, namely Yehovah's Spirit. Together, we are the body of Messiah— the dwelling place of Yehovah. We have his Torah written upon our hearts as our guide and his Spirit empowering us as we follow after the Messiah's example, rejecting rebellion and turning to a life of loyalty to the Creator. **(See 1 Corinthians 6:19-20; 1 Corinthians 3:16-17; Ephesians 2:21-22; Isaiah 66:1-2.)** In him, we die to our former ways and are gloriously reborn, grafted into his spiritual family as sons and daughters of God. I hope that you begin to see the magnitude of what this means. The Creator took upon himself the weaknesses of our fleshly bodies so that he could cover our insurmountable debts with his own blood. Through his willing, sacrificial death, he offers us life without end, and an unparalleled inheritance—to be called *Sons of God*. **(See John 1:12-13; Romans 8:14-23; Galatians 3:26; 1 John 3:1-2.)**

As his redeemed people, we respond to God's mercy by sanctifying ourselves through loyal obedience, submitting to the reality that his ways are higher and better than ours, and his wisdom is for our benefit. Our loyal faithfulness, therefore, is proof of our rebirth and trust-filled reliance in the ability of the Messiah to unite us back to the Creator. Though keeping God's commandments could never atone for our former wickedness and rebellion against God, by upholding them we acknowledge the reality that a redeemed life reflects the moral and ethical expectations of our Redeemer. As adopted sons and daughters, we take upon ourselves the reputation of Yehovah, agreeing to be his Imagers in the world. We bear his name by reflecting his nature, having been transformed by his Spirit.

I will leave you with one final thought. In one brief moment in history, the Messiah's death simultaneously abolished the sacrificial system, offered atonement once and for all to all who would trust in him, and extended inclusion into God's family to non-Jews everywhere. As profound as this good news is, it does not overshadow the many years spent by the Messiah on the earth wherein he taught us *how* to live. The two go hand in hand. There's a reason the Bible says far more about our conduct in this world than it does about our destination afterward. With this in mind, let's begin our journey into the Ten Commandments!

# From Sinai to Zion

Are you ready for an adventure? Imagine you are standing at the base of a large mountain in some faraway desert. You feel the ground beneath your feet begin to tremble as thick, dark clouds swirl above. A column of fire spirals downward, resting atop the mountain's peak. Lightning flashes all around, and you have to cover your ears as thunder rips across the sky.

It's like nothing you've ever seen, and no, it's not a scene from a movie. What I am describing actually happened over three thousand years ago at Mount Sinai. *Yehovah*, the Creator of the Universe, had heard the prayers of the Israelites, the descendants of Abraham, Isaac and Jacob, and had *mercy* on them. He had come to Egypt and saw his people were slaves to the cruel Egyptians, whom he had come to judge—along with their wicked gods. (**See Exodus 12:12.**) He was going to rescue the Israelites and bring them to the Promised Land. But first, he would take them to the mountain. There, he would give them the commandments and *teach* them how to behave. From that day onward, he was going to be their God and they would be his people.

Back in Egypt, Yehovah had come down to show that he was not like their gods. His power was unmatched, yet he was merciful and *good*, never forgetting a promise. He taught the Israelites that they could trust him. Unlike the *wicked* gods of Egypt, he was kind and just. At Mount Sinai, Yehovah gave the Israelites commandments that would guide them through life. They would bring *peace* between them and the Creator. But they would have to obey them if they wanted to stay in the land he was about to give them and live as members of his family.

Perhaps you're still wondering why you and I should care about the Ten Commandments, which are so old. It's a great question. But, in order to understand why they are important to us today, we have to realize that they were never random *laws* given to a group of people a long time ago by some angry god. They are the practical teachings given by the Creator so that we can live as he intended, and have peace with him and one another. In fact, *Yeshua* reminded us of the commandments by summarizing them one day when a teacher of the *Torah* asked him this question, "*Rabbi*, which is the greatest commandment in the Torah?"

Yeshua answered the teacher by quoting the Torah, saying, "Hear, O Israel: Yehovah our God, Yehovah is *one*. You shall love Yehovah your God with all your heart and with all your soul and with all your strength. This is the greatest and first commandment. And a second is like it: You shall love your neighbor as yourself. Upon these two commandments hang all the Torah and the Prophets."

In this book, we will learn exactly how the commandments protect us from what would otherwise destroy us. But first, it is important to know that keeping the commandments has never *saved* anyone, because that's not what they do. They can't cover over our *sins* any more than doing the right thing can erase the bad we've done wrong in the past. Think of it this way, Yehovah is perfect and his instructions are there to protect us from death. However, everyone who is old enough to make the choice has chosen at one time or another to rebel, deciding for themselves right and wrong instead of obeying the Creator. Because of this, we are separated from Yehovah, which means being separate from the giver of life. In this way, sin separates us from God and brings death. Thankfully, Yehovah knew we were weak and had a plan from the beginning.

He chose to become the bridge over that great divide that would keep us away from him by coming into the world in the body of a man named Yeshua. He would be our *Messiah*. But why? Think of it this way: Yehovah is perfect and is life, and our rebellion separates us from him and his life. This means that if we sin and he doesn't do something to rescue us, our very existence will end and we will die. The only way for God to protect the human race he created was for someone to die in our place. But who? No man was perfect, and so there wasn't anyone that could take our place. So Yehovah came in the body of a man, lived a life of perfect loyalty, and then died in our place. Through him, we are offered a way back to life. Yet, even though his death offers to cover over our sins, it doesn't stop us from continuing to live a life of wickedness and rebellion.

In the same way God rescued Israel from Egypt and then taught them to live as his people, the Messiah rescued the whole world from slavery to sin and taught us how to keep the commandments so that we would be at peace with Yehovah. This time, however, he would do something that had never been done before. He knew humans weren't strong enough to be perfectly loyal, so he offers to let his Spirit live within us, giving us the strength we will need to live as his people.

Do you remember the Exodus story? Maybe you read it before with your parents or heard about it in church. Perhaps this is your first time hearing it. Either way, in the story we read that God purchased the Israelites' freedom from the Egyptian pharaoh. As part of the deal, Yehovah told them that anyone who wanted to be part of God's family needed to do something. They would have to kill a spotless lamb and put its blood over the door of their homes. The blood would be a sign that told Yehovah that everyone inside belonged to him. When he came to destroy his enemies, he would stand over each home and protect his people from death. That event was called *Pesach*, because whenever God saw the blood, he stood over the doorway and protected the people inside. **(See Exodus 12.)**

After this, Yehovah *redeemed* Israel, leading them by the hand out of slavery and through the sea. Around fifty days later, the people arrived at Mount Sinai. That day is called *Shavuot*, and on it Yehovah came down in the most powerful way anyone had ever seen. He wrote his commandments on stone tablets to teach the whole nation how to live. Over a thousand years later, Yeshua was born. During his life, he never broke a single commandment and taught us exactly how to keep them fully.

He gave his life on Pesach, becoming our very own Pesach Lamb. He offered his blood to anyone who will place it over their hearts. Anyone who does will belong to Yehovah and will never experience death. Just like in the story of the exodus, Shavuot came fifty days after Yeshua was crucified. Once again, Yehovah sent something down on a mountain. This time, however, instead of writing the commandments on stone tablets, he sent his Spirit who wrote the Torah upon our hearts, dwelling in us and empowering us to overcome our mortal weakness and, by his strength, keep the commandments. **(See Jeremiah 31:31-34.)**

If that weren't enough, he promised to dwell within each of us so that we, and not some temple made of stones, would become the dwelling place of Yehovah on the earth! Unbelievably, there is more. Non-Jews everywhere were offered adoption into the family of Yehovah as sons and daughters in the greatest gift ever made to the world. We do not replace Israel. Instead, we would cause the borders of Yehovah's Kingdom to grow to the very ends of the Earth. Every human being on the planet was, for the first time, invited to become part of the body of the Messiah as *imagers* of the Creator—the dwelling place of Yehovah!

Back in Exodus, the story tells us of a man named Moshe—or Moses—whose name means "to draw out." In fact, Hebrew names often tell the story of the person to whom they belong. Moshe was not only drawn out of a river as a baby boy, but Yehovah used him as a man to draw the nation of Israel out of Egypt. Yet, despite all Moshe was, he was only a man. The *Deliverer* Yehovah was going to send would have to be perfect, and Yehovah had a plan. Remember, he wasn't just freeing Israel, but the entire world. And when Yehovah came to be our Messiah, he chose the name Yeshua. That name tells us his plan, as Yeshua means "Yehovah Delivers." This time, the Yehovah would do the rescuing himself.

The Ten Commandments are part of an agreement we have with the Creator. In the *covenant*, we receive redemption from slavery, the Spirit of Yehovah living within us, adoption as sons and daughters, and a life that never ends. We also have *shalom*, joy, *blessing*, protection, and access to our Father, the very Creator of life. All he asks from us is that we turn away from our former ways of wicked *rebellion*, trust in his ability to *cover* our sin, and live a new life of *loyal obedience* in which we spread his light and goodness into the world. In doing so, we die to our old ways and are reborn as his sons and daughters. No, it will not be easy. In fact, many have given their lives in the war against evil. But his Spirit empowers us, his Word renews our minds and his mercy is new every morning.

If you're still not sure about the commandments, just imagine what the world would look like if we kept them. There would be no theft, murder, kidnapping, violence, suffering, pain or wickedness. Imagine how peaceful the world would become in one day if we lived as he intended. The commandments aren't a burden. They exist to protect God's children from the things that cause pain, suffering, death, and destruction. If we would keep them, we would have peaceful relationships with the Creator and with one another, and we would flourish in the world he made.

In this book, we will dive into each of the Ten Commandments so we can explore what they meant to the Ancient Israelites when they were written. We will also learn what Yeshua the Messiah said about them, and begin to understand exactly God expects of his people. Each commandment is like a piece of a map. Together, they paint a picture of what is important to Yehovah, and help us navigate life with his wisdom and instruction. Are you ready to see the ancient words come to life? Let's go!

# The First Commandment

*"I am Yehovah your God who brought you out of the land of Egypt, from the house of slavery—you must never have for yourself other gods in my sight."*

The First Commandment begins in a loud, thunderous voice. Yehovah tells the Israelites that *he* was the one who redeemed them out of slavery. He heard their cries from Egypt and had mercy on them. His words remind us that he had not forgotten his promise to Abraham. (See Genesis 12.)

Hinting at what was to come, Yehovah provided Israel with a Deliverer (Moses) and lambs, whose blood would protect them from what was coming. Then, as Yehovah came down from heaven to make war against Egypt and its gods and kill the firstborn throughout the land, he saw the blood of the lamb on the doors. (See Exodus 12:12.) Each time he saw the blood, he knew the people inside belonged to him so he reached out his hand and protected them. This day was called *Passover*, and on it Yehovah showed both mercy and justice, guarding his *loyally obedient* people and striking down the wicked.

The First Commandment tells us that as God's family we're never allowed to engage with other gods. To be clear, the Ancient Israelites saw these *gods* as powerful spiritual beings, created by Yehovah, but not equal to him. Some of them chose to rebel against Yehovah and destroy humanity by having children with women and teaching men forbidden arts, hoping we would destroy ourselves and be punished by Yehovah. (See Genesis 6; The First Book of Enoch: Chapter 8.) Yehovah cast the ones that had children with humans into the Abyss. (See Jude 1:6-7; 2 Peter 2:4.)

When Yehovah brought the Israelites out of Egypt through the Sea, it was both practical and symbolic. All would know that Yehovah was unmatched in wisdom and power. Those in the Abyss were forced to watch their wicked plan unravel as Yehovah orchestrated the creation and redemption of a nation right in their faces, pulling humanity back from the brink.

The Israelites were led to Mount Sinai where Yehovah made a *covenant* with them. It was like a wedding, but instead of a husband and wife, Yehovah would be their God and they would be his people. As such, they would inherit his land—Canaan. But first, he would have to teach them how to stay there. Before they could enter this Promised Land, they would have to drive out the wicked people who were there worshiping rebel gods. The greatest test would be whether or not these Israelites would remain loyal.

By the end of the Exodus, Yehovah had done what only he could do. He made a family from a childless old man, Abram, and his barren wife, Sarai, who had come from the center of idol worship in Ur. He used Egypt to grow that family into a nation. Then, he brought Egypt and its gods to their knees, taught the Israelites how to be *righteous*, and used Israel to drive the wicked people from Canaan, the place where he would eventually come as the Deliverer to *redeem* the entire world.

In the first commandment, we see the seeds of a holy war against the spiritual rebels, and a coming immortal King who would take back all the nations. This Messiah would fulfill God's promise to Abraham to bless every nation through his children. As we remember the lengths to which our Father goes to keep his promises, we learn that we can *trust* him and worship him alone. We also learn not be like Pharaoh, who pridefully thought of himself as a god, doing as he pleased. Yehovah alone is worthy of our *worship*, trust and loyalty.

# The Second Commandment

*"You shall never make for yourself any carved image, a representation of anything in the skies above, in the earth below or what is in the waters under the earth. You shall not bow down to them or serve them..."*

Idolatry—worshiping, offering loyalty to or making agreements with spiritual beings other than Yehovah—is forbidden. It's easy to think we'd never do such a thing, but let's not forget about pride. Pride looks inwardly for guidance, following our deceptive hearts while rejecting Yehovah's ways. Pride puts us on the throne, exalts itself above Yehovah and tells us to choose for ourselves what is good. Pride rejects the Creator's commandments and says to do whatever is right in our own eyes. **(See Deuteronomy 12:8; Ezekiel 28:17; Isaiah 14:12-17.)** Yehovah will always humble the proud.

Whether it is through pride or idolatry, the Second Commandment prohibits worshiping anyone but Yehovah. Throughout history, people all over the world have interacted with spiritual beings by making statues and carvings that represented them. They didn't think the statues themselves were gods. Rather, they prayed to spiritual beings, or gods, asking them to come and enter the statues and listen to their requests. In exchange for healing, riches, secret knowledge, protection, or a curse on an enemy, the person offered their loyalty to that spirit, promising to do whatever it asked.

Yehovah commands us to never make such carved images. He doesn't even want his people interacting with wicked spiritual powers. They want one thing: our destruction.

Anyone in Yehovah's family found worshiping other gods was in serious trouble. The Creator knew they would eventually obey the wicked spirits and start doing evil, eventually causing everyone to forget Gods' Commandments, rebel and get kicked out of the Promised Land. This is why the Israelites were not even allowed to say the names of other gods or marry anyone who worshiped them.

Ever since Yehovah came in the flesh of a man as the Messiah to deliver the whole world from slavery to these wicked, rebel spirits, he offered us an escape from their destructive ways by offering us reconciliation, peace, and eternal life. For the first time in history, Yehovah offered every human being on the planet the opportunity to join his family! **(See Psalm 2:7-8; Isaiah 49:6; Psalm 98:2-3; Isaiah 45:22; Isaiah 56:6-8; Ephesians 2:11-22; Romans 11:1-32.)** As non-Jews who have joined Israel as citizens, having been adopted as sons and daughters of Yehovah, we must reject idolatry and pride, and loyally worship Yehovah alone.

# The Third Commandment

## *"You shall never bear the Name of Yehovah your God in emptiness."*

Your name and your reputation are the most valuable things you own, in that they carry the essence of who you are to the world. A reputation is sacred and should be protected. The Bible even says that a good name is more valuable than riches. **(See Proverbs 22:1.)** It's not hard to imagine that Yehovah takes his reputation seriously, too.

Since Yehovah is spirit and does not have a physical body, he relies on us to represent his values and character to the world. **(See Ezekiel 20:39.)** After all, we were created to be his imagers, ambassadors and priests here on the earth. **(See Genesis 1:26; 2 Corinthians 5:20; Revelation 1:5-6.)** With that in mind, if we bear—or take upon ourselves—the name of Yehovah, it means that we have chosen to represent the Creator. As his people, everything we do is a reflection of him. The Third Commandment is a warning. It tells everyone who belongs to Yehovah that they must take our responsibility seriously. If we reflect his reputation poorly, the consequences can be disastrous. It is serious business to be his ambassadors and imagers. We represent him well by being just, merciful, full of truth, kind, generous and morally upright. **(See Matthew 5:43-48; Luke 6: 27-26.)**

Before we take up the name of Yehovah and tell the world that we are his people, we must very carefully consider what that means, and be sure to do everything required, even when it's not easy. **(See Luke 14:27-33; John 14:15-24; 1 John 3:4-10.)** Being a loyal imager means dying to our ways so that he can live through us. **(See Deuteronomy 12:8.)** The God who created the universe and holds it in his hands is full of mercy and compassion, more humble than a servant, more generous than any man and perfectly honest. He upholds justice and defends the innocent. His words are always true and he moves heaven and earth to keep his promise. How are we doing so far? If you're anything like me, we have some work to do.

Just as the moon reflects the light of the sun back into a darkened world, as imagers of God we bear upon ourselves the name of Yehovah, reflecting his reputation, character, goodness and order like a beacon to a dark and broken world. It's a monumental task, no doubt, but the great news is that the Father offers to dwell within us to give us the strength and courage we need! **(See Ezekiel 36:27; John 14:23; Jeremiah 31:31-34; 1 Corinthians 2:10-13; Galatians 2:20.)**

# The Fourth Commandment

*"Remember to keep the Sabbath day set apart."*

The Fourth Commandment continues, *"Six days you shall labor, and do all your work, but the seventh day is a Sabbath to Yehovah your God. On it you shall not do any work, you, or your son, or your daughter, your male servant, or your female servant, or your livestock, or the foreign guest who is within your gates. Because in six days Yehovah made heaven and earth, the sea, and all that is in them, and rested on the seventh day. Therefore, Yehovah blessed the Sabbath day and made it holy."*

*Sabbath* is Hebrew for rest. The commandment tells us of a unique day which Yehovah created. He made it unique (*holy*) and caused it to *flourish*. The commandment is probably the most controversial of the ten. On this unique day, God's people are not allowed to work. Instead, they are commanded to rest, trusting that Yehovah is in control. In six days Yehovah created everything that we would need for seven days. In other words, the Sabbath was created to be our weekly reminder that our work does not make the world go round—he does.

When we pause and remember that Yehovah created the world in six days and holds the cosmos together, we realize that the Sabbath is his invitation for us to rest in confidence that he provides all we need. The Sabbath reminds us that we live in a world that runs on God's time, not ours. By keeping it separate, we not only show that we belong to him, but we remind ourselves that without him nothing functions as it should.

On Sabbath, Yehovah forbade work, such as gathering resources, carrying heavy things, as well as buying, selling, trading, or earning money. It was an abolition of both secular activities and conversation for twenty-four hours. But why does God seem to care? Simply put, Sabbath is a time to reflect on who God is and who we are not. On Sabbath, we reconnect with the Creator of the universe, spending time in worship, prayer, and reading the word. It is never intended as a burden, rather as a day we joyfully look forward to each week! It is supposed to be a day filled with delightful rest. In fact, Yeshua reminded us that the Sabbath was created for us, and that on the Sabbath we prioritize mercy and helping those in need.

The Sabbath has nothing to do with keeping man-made traditions or becoming self-righteous about how well we keep it, and it certainly isn't an excuse to avoid doing good or helping others. **(See Matthew 12:9-12.)** It's actually the opposite; a time to reset our watches to the Creator's clock. In humility, we put our trust in his capable and generous hands. In this way, there's no room for pride.

Since Yehovah wrote them on stone tablets at Sinai, people have bent the commandments to fit around their lifestyles, rather than bending their lifestyles to fit around the commandments. It should go without saying that pointing out a biblical worldview of the Sabbath is in no way advocating for an Orthodox Jewish approach with its own man-made traditions. However, by twisting Yehovah's words to fit what we want them to say is not only wrong, it's dangerous. As the body of Messiah and members of God's family, we should put our trust in Yehovah and humble ourselves to his ways. It's very easy in all this to lose sight of the purpose of the Sabbath, choosing instead to debate about what is or isn't permitted, or what day of the week it falls on. It should be enough to say that from the Creation until the Exodus, and onward through the lives of the Prophets, and even those of Yeshua and his apostles, Sabbath has never changed. Furthermore, Yeshua teaches us not to prefer man-made traditions over Yehovah's commandments. **(See Mark 7:1-13.)** It would be easier to stretch out your hand and touch the Sun than earn salvation by keeping the commandments, but that's not why they exist. Salvation is a merciful gift from the Creator. However, as God's sons and daughters, we obey his commandments, including Sabbath, as a way to demonstrate our loyal obedience to the One who not only delivered us, but provides all our needs each and every day.

# The Fifth Commandment

*"Honor your father and your mother, that your days may be long in the Land that Yehovah your God is giving you."*

We show respect to the Creator by honoring our father and mother—the man and woman through whom he brings us into the world. We should be asking what it means to honor someone. Does it mean to obey them, doing everything they ask? What if we don't know our mother or father, or have ungodly parents?

Let's look at the Hebrew word for honor and see what it means. Kabad is a special word that means much more than simply obey. Honoring our parents means "to place a heavy weight upon them." In other words, we should not take them or their role lightly. In fact, the word means "to glorify."

The word "honor" means something different to an Ancient Israelite than it did to a Roman. To the Israelite, honoring your father and mother meant to live in a way that casts a good light on their reputation. In other words, live your life in a manner worthy of the name your parents gave you. We should never bring shame on their reputation by our actions. In the same way that our choices reflect on the Creator, they also reflect upon our parents. So, we must remind ourselves that our actions affect more than our own lives. In this way, we honor the Creator and our parents by living a life of goodness— showing compassion, honesty, integrity, justice, and courage in everything we do. When our parents grow old, we take care of them in their weakness just as they took care of us in ours as babies. The Creator brought us into the world through them, so it is our responsibility to show them respect.

If you did not have the blessing of having good, god-fearing parents, you can still reflect the compassionate nature of your heavenly Father by honoring those that brought you into the world. Show them mercy and kindness, even if they showed you none. Ask the Father to bring someone into your life that can take on that role. And, when it's your turn to be the mother or father, offer your children your very best by teaching them Yehovah's love and kindness through your actions. If you had godly parents, be grateful for the blessing that not everyone had. Imitate what they taught you and reject any lifestyle that would dishonor their legacy.

# The Sixth Commandment

## *"You shall never murder."*

Yehovah formed *Adam* and placed him in the Garden of Eden. **(See Genesis 1:27; Genesis 2:5-8; Genesis 2:15.)** During creation, humanity was given the job of ruling over every living creature on the earth. We were to be his *imagers*. When Yehovah breathed his life into our lungs, he placed within each of us an incredibly precious gift, one that must be protected at all costs.

The Sixth Commandment teaches us that we cannot destroy that which we did not create. When someone takes a life it is the highest form of pride, cruelty, and rebellion against our Maker. A murderer puts his emotions and desires above God's will. He judges others as if he, a man, were God. The murderer rejects humility, believing his anger or desire for vengeance gives him the right to destroy one of Yehovah's imagers. Do you remember the spiritual rebels and what they tried to do? In their hatred for humanity they tried to destroy mankind. **(See Genesis 3; Genesis 6; Psalm 82.)** Being spiritual beings, there would be no redemption, and their punishment was severe and final. As for us, we cannot forget that all life comes from Yehovah, and only he can take it away, or establish rules for when death is the only appropriate punishment.

Before we assume we're innocent because we haven't murdered, Yeshua tells us that destroying someone's reputation is the same as killing them. **(See Matthew 5:21-26.)** We must pay careful attention to this commandment. You may never have imagined that humiliating someone or destroying their reputation was the same as taking a life—but the Creator sees them as equal. We are commanded to do to others as we want them to do to us, to reconcile our wrong doing, and live at peace with one another. And the hardest part is usually *reconciling*. Did you know the Bible never tells us to ask God to forgive us for the things we've done wrong to others? We are supposed to humble ourselves, go to the person and fix it.

If you stole, an apology to God wasn't required, and just saying sorry to the person wasn't enough. We are commanded to give back more than what we took. It's not just an *Old Testament* idea, either. **(See Luke 19:1-9; Matthew 5:23-24.)** The story of Zacchaeus tells us of when Yeshua met a dishonest tax collector. Read it for yourself and pay close attention to what the Messiah says after Zacchaeus pays back more than he stole.

The point is that God created every human being, and by destroying what God has made, either through words or violence, we directly oppose him. Yeshua told us that how we treat the least among us is how we treat the Messiah himself! (See Matthew 25:31-46.) So, be slow to anger, slow to speak, eager to forgive, run from gossip and evil speech as fast as you can, and love your neighbor as yourself and you will keep the Sixth Commandment.

# The Seventh Commandment

*"You shall never commit adultery."*

Adultery isn't a word we hear too often these days, but if we want to understand the heart of this commandment we first need to understand the importance of children in Ancient Israelite culture. In their world, as it often is in ours today, children represented a husband and wife's legacy and reputation. Children took their father's name and, in doing so, represented him and their ancestors in the community for the next generation. In turn, a father passed along all his wisdom and possessions with the hope that each generation might be better off than the one before.

Adultery certainly causes intense grief, but it is more than just breaking someone's heart. It places doubt in the authenticity of a man's children and legacy, which were considered as a blessing from the Creator. In this way, adultery robs a man of being part of a continued chain of humanity. But why? Simply put, it calls into question whether or not a child born by his wife is truly his. It certainly was not the case that all the blame for adultery was on the woman who participated. Quite the opposite. Anyone who willingly engaged in it was punished for breaking the sacred covenant of marriage. **(See Leviticus 20:10; Deuteronomy 22:25-27.)** In the case of rape, the criminal—not the victim—was sentenced to death.

Sexual relationships between anyone besides a husband and wife caused a wave of destruction that could last for generations. Any man who took another man's wife not only invaded the sacred covenantal space that did not belong to him, but he brought chaos to the entire community by destroying the trust that was supposed to exist between neighbors, and creating painful consequences for many years to come.

Adultery was also used to describe God's people anytime they worshiped other gods. When Yehovah saw his people break their covenant with him, he was hurt and angered, like a husband who witnessed his own wife in the arms of another lover. He had done everything for them. Still, they snuck away to worship wicked gods who wanted to destroy them.

In the ancient world, having multiple wives was not uncommon. It was often practiced by the wealthy and powerful for creating alliances and heirs. Many times a man could take multiple wives in order to provide for a widow who might otherwise starve or be unable to carry on her late husband's name. **(See Deuteronomy 25:5.)** This was not considered adultery and was accepted, so long as the husband met all his duties. **(See Exod 21:10.)** However, God had always intended for a husband to have one wife from the beginning, as we see in the Garden of Eden. In fact, when God chose a man to create the nation of Israel, he chose Abraham, a man with one wife. It was when he had a child with his wife's servant, Hagar, that he created a problem that would plague his descendants for generations.

By the time Yeshua arrived on the scene, having multiple wives became common. In fact, elders and overseers were prohibited from the practice in the New Testament. As was often the case, Yeshua taught us that behind every wicked act is a thought. Like seeds into fruit, our thoughts grow into actions. If those thoughts are wicked, it won't be long until our actions are as well. For this reason, Yeshua places the burden on the man when he says that anyone who desires another man's wife has already committed adultery with her in his heart. **(See Matthew 5:27-32.)** We must take the destructive potential of adultery seriously and remove it completely from our minds. **(See Proverbs 5.)** Thankfully, Yehovah offers to empower us with his Spirit! **(See Ezekiel 36:26-27; Galatians 5:16-25; John 14:15-23.)**

# The Eighth Commandment

## *"You shall never steal."*

*Ganav* is Hebrew for "to steal." Yet, the word means so much more. It means "to deceive," "to defraud," "to swindle," "to practice falsehood," and even... "to kidnap." A thief is someone who takes what does not belong to him. By doing so, he puts his desires above his neighbor's right to keep what he has earned. A thief's words are empty because he uses them to convince his victims while he escapes with what is theirs. A thief lives as if he will never face judgment for his actions. **(See Proverbs 1:8-19.)**

Charging too much interest is called "usury." Unlike the thief who sneaks around in the dark, usury is often found in a more formal setting, but it is no less wicked. Usury takes advantage of the poor, enslaving them with debt. **(See Leviticus 25:35-37.)** Lying, cheating on agreements, not paying workers, or tricking others by using faulty measurements breaks a fundamental trust that must exist between people. **(See Deuteronomy 24:14-15, Leviticus 19:35-36.)** These actions start a chain-reaction that makes everyone suspicious of one another. Generosity turns into greed and theft ruins friendships, causing hatred and tearing communities apart. Ganav is rebellion against Yehovah and brings chaos. **(See John 10:10.)**

There were two thieves on either side of Yeshua during his crucifixion. They stood as an example of our guilt when compared to the innocence of the Messiah. One thief humbled himself, while the other did not. Yehovah offers mercy to the one who humbles himself, but judgement to those who practice ganav. **(See 1 Corinthians 6:9-11; Revelation 22:15.)**

Today, we see the effects of theft everywhere—but imagine a world without it: no suffering from human trafficking, slavery or kidnapping. No financial crashes, locked doors, safes, passwords, security guards or even cameras. Neighbors would share in time of need. Ganav is like a rock dropped into a calm pool of water. It affects everything it touches, spreading its chaos. Yehovah's imagers push back through honesty, generosity and integrity. In other words, "Whatever you wish that others would do to you, do also to them, for this is the Torah and the Prophets." **(See Matthew 7:12.)**

# The Ninth Commandment

### *"You shall never give a deceitful testimony against another."*

The Ninth Commandment is about truth and justice, two things that define the character of the Creator. Unlike Lady Justice, Yehovah is not blind. Quite the opposite, in fact. He sees everything. In order to understand the Ninth Commandment, we need to know what it means to be a *witness*. A witness is someone who knows the truth about an event because they saw it happen with their own eyes. A judge might ask the witness to explain what happened so he can be sure there is justice. A false witness is someone who knows the truth, but chooses to lie. Their words can have a lasting effect. Sadly, the words of a false witness are worse than a lie. They are the enemy of the truth. They don't only avoid justice, they turn it upside down.

A false witness may lie for many reasons: to hurt someone they don't like, to protect a guilty person they love, to get out of trouble themselves, or maybe just to get something they want. In any case, innocence has no value to the false witness. Their words are like poison, injecting chaos and destruction into a community. They can even send an innocent person to their death. Needless to say, Yehovah takes this very seriously. He hates the false witness. (**See Proverbs 6:19.**) The Torah teaches us that if a witness is caught lying, they must receive the exact same punishment that an innocent person was about to receive, had the witness not been caught lying. (**See Deuteronomy 19:16-19.**)

The world only works as God intended it to when his people seek truth, justice and mercy like he does. (**See Psalm 31:5; Deuteronomy 32:4; Psalm 89:14; Isaiah 30:18; Exodus 34:6-7.**) A false witness replaces these things with selfishness, bribes and lies. Their words corrupt society, condemn the innocent and let the guilty go free. They invert the truth, and have no place amongst God's people. (**See Leviticus 19:15; Revelation 21:8.**)

Yeshua upheld the Ninth Commandment, emphasizing honesty. (**See Matthew 19:18; Matthew 5:33-37.**) In fact, there were several priests that used the lies of false witnesses to accuse the Messiah of sin because they wanted to murder him. (**See Matthew 26:59-61; Mark 14:55-59.**) The same thing happened with Stephen. So, whether they mean to or not, false witnesses join spiritual rebels in opposing the will of the Creator. (**See Acts 6:11-14.**) As for the body of Messiah, we must be honest, just, merciful, and never afraid of the truth. (**See 1 John 3:21-22; Proverbs 10:9.**)

# The Tenth Commandment

*"You shall not covet your neighbor's house; you shall not covet your neighbor's wife, or his male servant, or his female servant, or his ox, or his donkey, or anything that is your neighbor's."*

A good way to understand the word "covet" is to think of it like having a deep "desire." Of course, it's not wrong to want something that you don't have, unless it's something that already belongs to someone else. In fact,

it's good to want a godly spouse, a healthy family, a home, and a meaningful job. However, wanting someone else's family, house, or job is forbidden. Desires like that can quickly spread until they take over your mind.

In the Torah, there's a story about Adam's firstborn son, Cain. (**See Genesis 4:1-7.**) In the story, Cain and his brother, Abel, offer gifts to Yehovah. Abel brings his best, but Cain offers something ordinary, so Yehovah only accepts Abel's gift. Cain wanted Yehovah to accept his offering, too, but he wasn't willing to do what his brother did to gain God's favor. He could have easily admitted that he hadn't given his best and fixed the problem.

Instead, he chose to murder his brother. Just before he did, Yehovah came to him and warned him that an evil force was waiting for the chance to destroy him. The force was called *sin*, and Yehovah told Cain that he must rule over it. Sadly, Cain didn't listen. Within a few years, mankind went from living peacefully in the Garden of Eden, to living in a world filled with murder, pain, and suffering.

Desiring what already belongs to someone else is like a virus that infects the mind. **(See 2 Corinthians 10:3-5.)** In fact, Yeshua points out that it is these inner desires that are often the real problem. **(See Matthew 5:27-28.)** As members of God's family, there's no room for coveting what belongs to someone else. **(See Philippians 4:8-9; Romans 12:1-2.)**

We keep the Tenth Commandment and win the battle over our minds by casting down every desire that opposes Yehovah, and finding joy when others are blessed. By doing this, our thoughts begin to reflect our new lives in the Messiah as *sons of God*. There's nothing we need that our Father hasn't already done. He's already redeemed us from death, adopted us into his family, and offered to fill us with his Spirit. It's safe to say that we can trust him to provide everything we need! **(See Matthew 6:25-33; 1 John 3; Revelation 3:17-21.)**

# Where do we go from here?

Like everyone who has ever come before us, we each have to decide for ourselves if we will choose loyal obedience to Yehovah. Or, like Adam and Eve did in the Garden of Eden, we can reject the Father's wisdom and choose to redefine good and evil for ourselves. Every day the choice is inevitable, and it is ours alone to make. As you make yours, I'll leave you with one final verse that I hope will help guide you in your decision.

*"Pay close attention, I have set before you today life and good, death and evil. If you obey the commandments of Yehovah your God that I command you today, by loving Yehovah your God, by walking in his ways, and by keeping his commandments and his statutes and his rules, then you shall live and multiply, and Yehovah your God will cause you to flourish in the land which you go to inherit. But, if your heart turns away, and you will not hear, but are drawn away to worship other gods and serve them, I declare to you today, that you shall surely be destroyed. You shall not live long in the land that you are going over the Jordan to enter and inherit. I call heaven and earth to witness against you today, that I have set before you life and death, blessing and curse. Therefore choose life, that you and your offspring may live, loving Yehovah your God, obeying his voice and holding fast to him, for he is your life and length of days, that you may dwell in the land that Yehovah swore to your fathers, to Abraham, to Isaac, and to Jacob, to give them." Deuteronomy 30:15-20*

# QUES

1. Which came first, the exodus from Egypt, or the Ten Commandments at Sinai?

2. Which commandment deals with our thoughts?

3. What does Yehovah think about pride?

4. What are we supposed to do if we sin against someone?

5. Is gossip really that bad?

6. What does the word "repent" really mean?

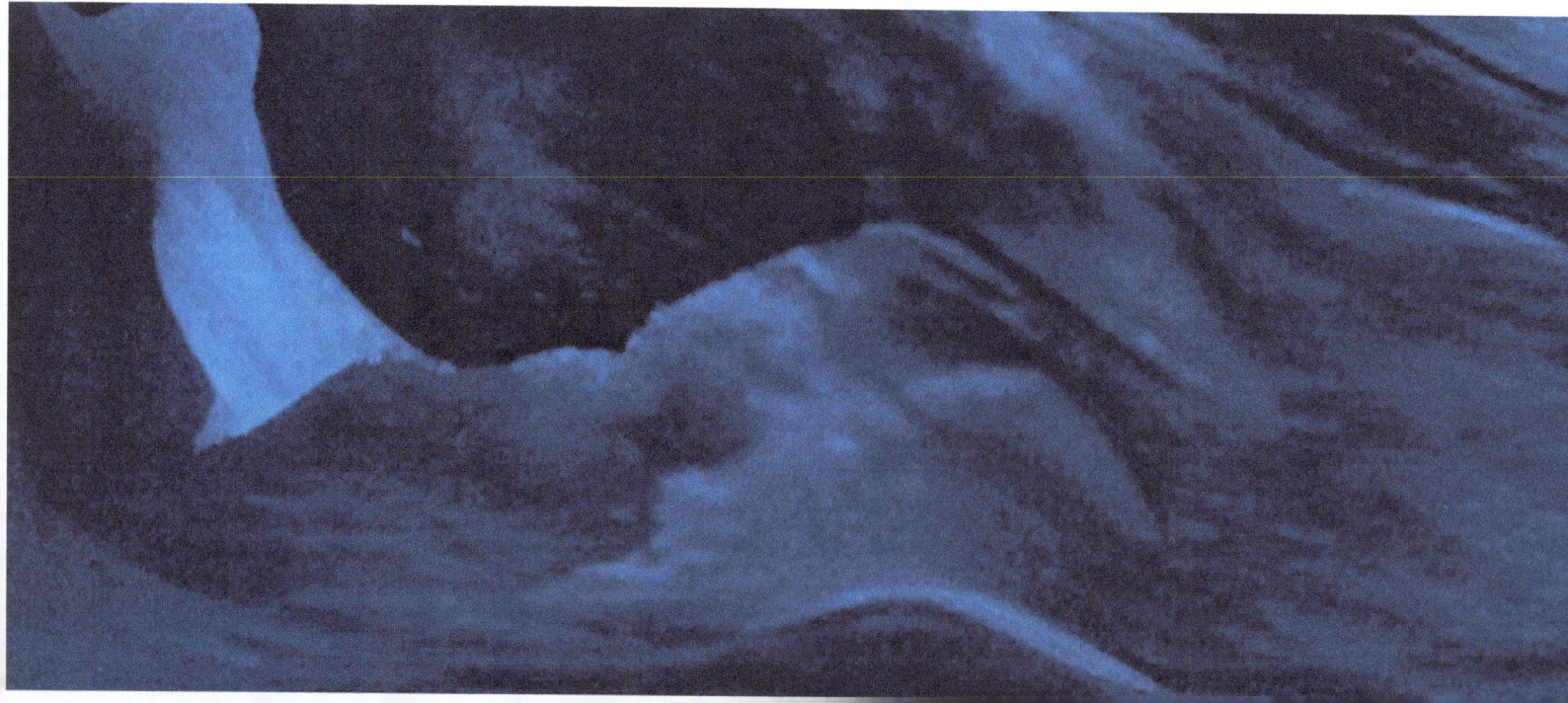

# TIONS

7. *How do we show Yehovah that we love him?*

8. *What are two reasons the Messiah came?*

9. *Why is life so important to Yehovah?*

10. *Are we supposed to keep all of the Ten Commandments today?*
*Even the Sabbath?*

*(For answers, see page 30.)*

1. God redeemed Israel before ever giving them the Ten Commandments at Mt. Sinai, which teaches us two things. The first is that salvation was never something we could earn. It also teaches us that dismissing the Ten Commandments simply because keeping them won't save us greatly misunderstands their purpose. The Ten Commandments have always been God's moral standard, instructing those that have already been redeemed how to live upright. As Yeshua said, "Therefore whoever breaks one of the least of these commandments and teaches others to do the same will be called least in the kingdom of heaven, but whoever keeps them and teaches them will be called great in the kingdom of heaven." -Matthew 5:19

2. The Tenth Commandment deals with desiring what belongs to someone else. Coveting exists in our minds and, if we don't control it, will control us. Think of it like a wild vine that destroys everything it touches. Before spreading its roots and choking out everything in its path, it starts as a tiny seed. It's much easier to remove that tiny seed before it grows than it is to fix the destruction left by the wild plant.

3. Proverbs 6:16-19 tells us, "there are six things Yehovah hates, seven which are an abomination to him." The first thing mentioned is pride. Why? Pride blinds us to the reality that we are neither immortal nor all that powerful, yet we have the audacity against the One who breathed life into our lungs and knitted each of us together in our mother's womb. Yehovah, on the other hand, is more humble than we can imagine. The Creator of the universe came to the world that he made in the weak, mortal body of a baby so he could serve us, teach us and take the punishment for our rebellion. (See John 13:1-17; Matthew 20:20-28.) So tell me, who on earth is like our God who responds to the wicked with mercy, the proud with humility and the stubborn with patience!

4. Yehovah desires reconciliation more than we realize. (See Romans 5:10-11; John 3:16-21.) It is the nature of Yehovah to bring order into chaos, light into darkness, and peace to suffering. When we sin against someone, an apology to God doesn't bring reconciliation. Why not? Because it's our responsibility as God's imagers to restore what we have broken, as much as it is possible to do so. (See Matthew 5:23-24; Luke 19:1-10; Leviticus 6:1-7.) Leave no stone unturned in seeking peace with God and others, because the peacemakers will be called the Sons of God. (See Matthew 5:9.)

5. Yeshua compares public humiliation to murder. Gossip and slander destroy a good reputation, divide people, and can crush a spirit that was created by God himself. Every word we say is recorded and we will have to give an account for everything we say. If evil lives in our hearts, it will come out of our mouths. (See Psalm 139:23-24; Romans 12:1-21.) So as God's imagers, we must be filled with compassion and brotherly love, speak well of others, refuse to take part in gossip and evil speech, reconcile our differences, and make peace.

6. The Hebrew word for "repent" is teshuvah, and means "to turn." Unlike the Latin word "poenitire" from which we get the word "repent," teshuvah is not an emotional state of being. It is a transforming action. Teshuvah has nothing to do with feeling regret or apologizing. It is the act of turning away from the things that you were doing that oppose God, and returning to his ways that bring life. Like we find in the story of Zacchaeus, part of the process of turning back to God is reconciling the things we've done wrong to others.

7. We don't show love with emotional words or songs about our affection. As beautiful as those forms of expressions can be, love (ahav) has nothing to do with a feeling. It is about covenantal loyalty. Biblical love is a choice to obey, honor, serve, and worship the Creator, aligning ourselves to his ways and reflecting his nature in our lives. As his imagers, we demonstrate love not with our words, but by reflecting his character in our actions and bringing his kingdom everywhere we go.

8. The Messiah came to show us how to live. The blood of the Passover lamb in Exodus was shed to mark the people who belonged to Yehovah so that death couldn't enter their homes. When God saw that blood, he knew the people inside belonged to him, so he protected them from death. Yeshua is our Passover Lamb, and his blood marks us as belonging to the Father. Anyone marked with the blood of the Messiah will never taste death, but will inherit the promise of eternal life.

9. Yehovah is the giver of life and in him there is no death. As his sons and daughters, we respect his supreme authority. If he creates a life, its value is beyond measure and belongs to him. We have no authority to destroy it, unless he specifically gives us that authority in the Word of God. If each human being is an imager of Yehovah, whatever we do to one another we do to him. (See Matthew 25:31-46.)

10. The answer is yes. Even though keeping the Ten Commandments cannot ever earn salvation, not one of the Ten Commandments was ever abolished or changed. Yeshua makes this clear. (See Matthew 5:17-20.) Paul's words to a mixed community of Jews and Gentiles are also clear. (See 1 Corinthians 7:17-19.) Gentile followers of Yeshua have been grafted into God's family as sons and daughters, and citizens of Israel. Having been born again through the resurrection of the Messiah, we both bear his name and keep his commandments, aligning ourselves to his appointed times and acknowledging his provision. (See Colossians 2:16.)

# Glossary

**Adultery** (*na'aph*): To have sexual relations with a betrothed or married person. In layman's terms, it means to break or cause to be broken a covenant that was made that binds two people together in marriage, or the promise of marriage. It is the human equivalent to idolatry, wherein someone abandons their covenant with Yehovah in order to apostatize (to turn away from Yehovah) and instead engage with another god. It is the opposite of love (*ahav*), or covenantal loyalty.

**Atonement** (*kippur*): See Reconcile.

**Belief** (*emunah*): From the root verb *aman*, meaning "to believe." In Hebrew, belief implies more than an idea to which one subscribes, as in a theological or intellectual stance. *Emunah* can be understood as one's loyalty, reliability, trustworthiness, or faithfulness. It recognizes the supreme authority, wisdom and goodness of the Creator, requiring demonstrable loyalty on the part of the created. (See Isaiah 55:6-9; James 2:14-26.) Therefore, biblical belief is an understanding firmly rooted in our willingness to act upon what we know to be true. Perhaps a more practical definition for belief may be "loyal faithfulness."

**Bless** (*barak*): To kneel, as in to honor. When Yehovah blesses someone or something, the direct result is that the recipient of that honor flourishes. An Ancient Israelite way of understanding blessing has nothing to do with a divine being causing fate to realign itself in our favor. Perhaps a more accurate way to think of blessing would be to first recognize that Yehovah created the entire world to function in a particular way, like an ecosystem. When we function in life the way Yehovah intended, we connect ourselves to an ecosystem that causes us to flourish by design. For example, God created a system we call the *Hydrologic Cycle* that brings freshwater to lands far from bodies of water. Without this system, the Earth would be inhospitable to life. When a seed is planted in the ground near a river, its roots grow deep and connect to the water source. If, however, a seed tries to grow in a desert where there is no water, it will die. In the same way, when we function as God intended, there is a natural flourishing that will occur. For example, by showing generosity toward the poor, we create a system that not only ensures none suffers needlessly, but exists in our own time of need. Or, by simply demonstrating faithfulness in one's marriage, we create stability for future generations, encourage trust, reduce jealousy and violence, and increase joy and a sense of belonging. On the other hand, greed and infidelity breed distrust, suspicion, hatred, murder, pain and suffering. So, instead of thinking of blessing and cursing as external forces out of our hands, think of them as a direct reflection of our choice to either align ourselves with Yehovah's system, or in opposition to it.

**Commandment** (*mitzvah*): An instruction, rule or order given by the Creator. The commandment acts as a barrier of protection—like a guardrail—separating the one who follows it from the destruction and chaos found outside its protection.

**Covenant** (*berit*): A binding pledge, agreement, promise, or contract; from Hebrew *kārat* ("to cut")—literally, "to cut a covenant." In Ancient Near Eastern treaties, parties would cut an animal in half and walk between the pieces, saying, "May this happen to me if I break the oath." Breaching the covenant, therefore, meant death. In **Genesis 15**, Yehovah does something profound. He puts Abraham to sleep and passes between the pieces *alone*. This is significant, in that Yehovah bound himself by an oath to fulfill a promise, which included a blessing to all nations through him. If Abraham or his offspring were to fail in being blameless, as required in **Genesis 17**, Yehovah would bless the nations anyway. Specifically, Yehovah would come to the earth born as a man, namely Yeshua the Messiah. As the offspring of Abraham and also Yehovah's essence in human form, he would take upon himself the punishment for man's rebellion. In this way, we can place our trust in the Messiah's sacrifice, bringing us back into right standing with the Creator. Yet, for our part, we must be wholeheartedly loyal to Yehovah and blameless. (See Matthew 5:48; Deuteronomy 18:13.) Thankfully, the Creator offers to empower us with his Spirit so we can walk in his ways. (See Ezekiel 36:26-27.)

**Covet** (*chamad*): To desire, want, or take pleasure in something or someone. In the context of the Tenth Commandment, it is forbidden to desire something or someone that is bound to someone else. Instead of desiring what belongs to another, we should rejoice when Yehovah causes others to flourish. Still, it is not wrong to work hard and earn something that we want, so long as we obtain it in an upright way and not by cheating, stealing, or deception, or desiring something that already belongs to someone else. Coveting is a seed, a thought or a feeling, that, if not uprooted quickly, turns into wicked, destructive behavior.

**Curse** (*arar*): To pronounce a binding (divine) verdict that dooms the offender to loss of life, fruitfulness, and favor, placing them under God's active opposition and withdrawal of blessing; the opposite of blessing. The effect of the curse is that those who rebel against Yehovah remove themselves from the source of life, as was the case with Adam and Eve in the Garden, or Cain as he farmed the land. When Cain rebelled by killing his brother, the land would no longer produce as it had before. (See Genesis 4:12.) God's judgement for rebellion is usually accomplished through famine, drought, pestilence, natural disasters, disease, etc. The goal of the curse is usually to force the offender to recognize the error and turn back to God's ways and reconcile.

**Deliver** (*yasha*): To save, deliver, rescue, or help. To cause someone to be free.

**Desire:** See Covet.

**Disciple** (*talmid*): Student, pupil or scholar; from the Hebrew *lamad*, meaning, "to learn" or "to be trained" as a sheep is trained by its shepherd. In Judea, every student needed a teacher, or *rabbi*, in order to learn. Students were expected to know, understand and follow the teachings of their rabbi. (See Deuteronomy 6:4-9.) As followers of the Messiah, Yeshua is *our* rabbi and he commanded us to go and make students of the pagan world, not simply converts to a particular denomination, but genuine followers of Messiah who are loyal to Yehovah. For more, see *Rabbi*.

**Echad** (one): More than just a numeric value, it denotes absolute oneness—complete, whole, indivisible, and lacking nothing. *Echad* is not a collective unity or an agreement between two things, rather a singular thing in its very essence. (See Deuteronomy 6:4.) In John 10:30 and John 17:21, the Messiah and Yehovah are one, which only requires modalism if one takes a flawed and dramatically narrow view of the omnipresence of Yehovah, who can simultaneously dwell in mankind (John 14:23; Isaiah 57:15; Jeremiah 23:23-24; 1 Kings 8:27; John 14:8-11) and be on the throne. In Greek, *heis* and *hen* likewise express this absolute oneness, without inherent plurality or collective unity. Thus, the Messiah is the physical incarnation of the invisible Yehovah who was made flesh to tabernacle amongst humanity, so that we might see the splendor of the Yehovah and survive the encounter. He was also born into a body because it was necessary that his body die. In this way, the undefinable essence and uncontainable majesty of Yehovah is one with Yeshua the Messiah. There was a distinction in role, but inseparability in nature and being.

**Evil (*ra'a*):** To break into pieces; spoil; do wickedly; be displeasing. *Ra'a* is dysfunction and the shattering of harmony. Perhaps an easier way to understand it is in its relationship to sin, or *chata*. *Chata* is the act itself of straying from the path, while *ra'a* is the consequent harm or chaos that follows. For instance, imagine an archer standing in a forest. Using his training, the archer takes aim, intending to send his arrow down a particular path towards the target. If the arrow deviates from the path, it misses the target and scatters. In Hebrew, *moreh* means both archer and teacher. It comes from *yarah*, which means to throw, to shoot, to instruct or to teach. In this way, a teacher is like an archer. Instead of aiming arrows, a teacher aims people. The path is that of life, the instruction is Torah and the target is a meaningful and upright life. (**See Psalm 127:3-5.**) An arrow that misses the mark (*chata*), shatters into pieces (*ra'a*). The thematic contrast between chaos and order is present in the Ancient Israelite mind, one that is vivid in **Deuteronomy 30:15–19**, wherein Moses sets before Israel life and good, death and evil, with Torah as the guide.

*Note: Many Ancient Egyptians worshiped a sun god that went by the name Ra. There is no known etymological link between it and the Proto-Semitic root for ra'a', thus any connection is purely thematic in nature. It is certainly possible that phonetic resemblance might have carried some cultural weight, as the Ancient Israelites would have been familiar with the prominent Egyptian deity, as well as its more engaged counterpart, Hathor, otherwise known as the "Eye of Ra," that existed during their slavery in Egypt. The near-perfect inversion of the Hebraic understanding of ra'a' as dysfunction and chaos, and the Egyptian definition of Ra as the god of creation and order is intriguing as a possible polemic. However, it is likely coincidental, albeit one which is magnified by the Israelites' worship of the golden calf at Sinai, likely representing Hathor. Hathor was tasked with protecting Egypt during conquests across the sea, and protecting Pharaoh and Egypt during campaigns beyond its borders. As such, the overlap begs the question: was there any link in the Ancient Israelite mind between ra'a' and Ra? The honest answer is that I don't know, but my contention is that the Ancient Israelites seldom missed a good opportunity for polemic wordplay.*

**Faith:** See Belief.

**Flourish:** See Bless.

**Follow (*halak achar*):** To go (as in "to follow") after; accompany. (**See Deuteronomy 13:4; 1 Kings 14:8; Numbers 32:15.**) The phrase means more than simply declaring an ideological alliance; it denotes a life of loyal devotion in which one has been joined in subservience and allegiance to another. The Greek word *akoloutheó*, which means "to follow or accompany," is found ninety times throughout the synoptic gospels. (**See Matthew 16:24.**)

**Forgive (*calach*):** To forgive or pardon, as in "to release or let go." In the Hebrew mind, Yehovah is not only Creator, but the Judge who precisely and meticulously maintains a record of every human action, word and even thought. Every good deed and every transgression is recorded. Despite this, Yehovah is ready, willing and quick to forgive those who turn from their wickedness and follow his ways. (**See Ezekiel 18:21-29.**) His promise to those who faithfully return to his ways is that the record of their wrongdoing is blotted out and all their debts are forgiven. The Greek equivalent is *aphiémi*. (**See Matthew 18:21-35.**)

**Gentiles (*goyim*):** Non-Hebrew people; generally, the nations. The term often implies pagan peoples who did not follow Torah. The Good News announced that these Gentiles were now invited to join God's family through the Messiah's work—adopted as sons of God and citizens of Israel. All men are created by Yehovah, and as such there is no hierarchy of value between them. Yet, in Messiah there is no longer distinction in status between Jews and Gentiles. A Jew is now one inwardly, in terms of loyalty to Yehovah and his Messiah, and circumcision is of the heart. That is to say, those who were once separated from Yehovah for their wicked rebellion are now, by trusting in his Messiah, grafted into Israel as sons and citizens, not to replace it, but to expand its borders. (**See Psalm 82:8.**) The Mosaic Covenant had been replaced with a New Covenant—its only fault being that man broke it. (**See Jeremiah 31:31-34.**) Its sacrificial system and priesthood had kept mankind at peace with Yehovah for generations, but merely foreshadowed a greater Messianic reality, one in which Yehovah took on the flesh in order to bear the punishment of our transgressions. He died once for all. Through this Great High Priest, the remnant of Israel became a kingdom of priests, their circumcision of the heart as was originally intended. (**See Deuteronomy 30:6; Exodus 19:6.**) The transfer of priesthood from Aaron's lineage to all followers of the Messiah, both ethnically Jewish and Gentile, does not abolish the Commandments—rather, Torah is now written on the heart. (**Jeremiah 31:33; Ezekiel 36:26–27.**)

**God (*elohim*):** *Elohim* is the plural form of the less common form *eloah*, meaning "mighty one." It is used to denote one or more spiritual powers, or "gods." The term can be either generic or specific, depending on its usage. *Elohim* can be understood as a place of residence term, wherein human beings are bound to a physical world by way of our physical bodies, non-human, spiritual beings do not reside in the physical world, and are thus broadly *elohim*. The term is primarily, though not exclusively, used by biblical authors to refer to Yehovah, the Creator. The distinction between meanings is established in the grammar and context of each verse.

**Good (*tov*):** To be pleasing, good, or doing well, as in thriving or flourishing; the opposite of dysfunction. In other words, to properly function as intended by the Creator, thus in alignment with the created order of things.

**Holy (*qadash*):** Set apart or dedicated for divine purpose; to be morally and/or ceremonially pure; by extension, not engaged in rebellion, wickedness, perversion, pollution, corruption, defilement, or dysfunction.

**Honor (*kabad*):** To be heavy, as in to place a great burden of importance upon something. In the Fifth Commandment, *kabad* suggests that instead of bringing shame or dishonor upon our parents' reputation through immorality, we realize the gravity of their position in bringing life into the world on behalf of the Creator, and we honor their reputation with upright conduct and by caring for our parents in the weakness of old age as they leave this world, just as they cared for us in the weakness of infancy when we entered it.

**Humility (*'anavah*):** A posture taken reflecting the reality of our status in the world as mortal, weak and dependent beings, particularly in light of the unmatched splendor and might of the Creator. In other words, humility is the state of being truly self-aware, understanding that neither pride nor arrogance can exist amongst God's sons and daughters, since it has no place in him. He who made the universe came to serve mortal men. The Maker of the hosts of heaven humbled himself and took upon our weakness. If that were not enough, he bore also our guilt, and then our death, which, of all things, came at the hands of his creation. In all this, he showed unparalleled mercy. As his sons, we are to reflect his nature in all we do. Humility is not to be confused with self-hatred, humiliation or self-deprivation. Rather, it is the recognition that worship belongs to Yehovah alone and his wisdom is high above our own.

**Imager:** Term used to signify someone who represents Yehovah. In other words, an imager is an ambassador, or representative, of Yehovah who carries his message and does his work on the earth. Imagers have the Creator's blessing, as well as the burden of responsibility to reflect his essence in an honorable manner. For more, read *The Unseen Realm* by Dr. Michael S. Heiser.

**Law (*Torah*):** Instruction or teaching; the first five books of the Bible—Genesis, Exodus, Leviticus, Numbers, Deuteronomy—are traditionally referred to as *HaTorah*, or "the Torah." However, the collective title refers not to the teachings *of* Moses, but the teachings of Yehovah as delivered *by* Moses. The Greek *nomos* ("law") is the Septuagint's standard rendering, but in English "law" offers a harsh connotation, failing to convey the intimate nature of *Torah* as the instructions a father offers his children to guide and protect them from mortal danger. The *Torah* contains civil codes, an outline for a sacrificial system, histories, covenants, polemics, lineages, commandments, requirements for a priesthood, and much more. The complex nature complicates the simplistic usage of the term. At its core, *Torah's* essence is as Yehovah's teaching. In his letter to Rome, Paul uses *nomos* flexibly, most often referring to some element of the *Torah*, such as the sacrificial system, though in many instances he uses *nomos* to refer to a legalistic distortion of it. Simply put, there was no salvation possible by keeping all the commandments. Israel was redeemed prior to Sinai. In fact, redemption has always been an act of Yehovah's mercy. **(See Nehemiah 9:27-28; Exodus 6:5.)** Paul also uses *nomos* as metaphor for a governing principle, as in a philosophical sense, (e.g., "law of sin and death," **(See Romans 8:2.)** The Sinai Covenant, which is part of the Torah, was broken by Israel. So, Yehovah promised a New Covenant to the House of Israel and the House of Judah. **(See Jeremiah 31:31–34.)** This time, Torah was written by the Spirit of God onto hearts, rather than stone tablets. **(See 2 Corinthians 3:3.)** Yehovah's people are no longer under the previous covenant's jurisdiction, nor are they saved by self-righteousness, but once again by Yehovah's merciful redemption. Torah's moral standard remains Yehovah's eternal will, intensified in the New Covenant. Yeshua's sacrifice and eternal priesthood do not nullify Torah—they empower obedience for the body of Messiah to become the dwelling place of Yehovah. This call for a kingdom of priests **(See 1 Peter 2:9)** is a universal invitation for humanity to join Yehovah's family as sons of God. Torah is the standard, not the solution. In this way, Yehovah's mercy does not lower the bar. Instead, it provides the Spirit of God himself living in the hearts of men as the power needed to keep it. In short, Torah is the Father's instruction—revealed at Sinai, broken by Israel, renewed in Messiah, and empowered by the Spirit.

**Lawless (*bliya`al*):** Literally, "without yoke" or "without instruction," whereas *beliy* is "without" and *ya'al* is "benefit, yoke, instruction." It describes the state of rejecting Yehovah's Torah, resulting in worthlessness, chaos, and rebellion against divine order **(See Deuteronomy 13:13; 1 Samuel 2:12; Proverbs 6:12.)** The verb *pāsha'* is conceptually related, though etymologically unique—its root meaning "to break away" or "revolt," emphasizing the deliberate act of covenant breach **(See Isaiah 53:5; Psalm 32:1.)** In the Septuagint (LXX), *pāsha'* is often rendered *anomia*, linking it to *bliya`al*. The Greek *anomia* derives from *nomos* "law" and the prefix *a-* meaning "without." In this way, *anomia* means "without law"—or more precisely—"without Torah." In the New Testament, *anomia* describes active wickedness that turns away from Yehovah's instruction. **(See Matthew 7:23; 13:41; 24:12; 1 John 3:4.)** Paul contrasts *anomia* with the life led by the Spirit of Yehovah, and equates *Belial* with ultimate lawlessness. **(See 2 Corinthians 6:14-15; Romans 6:19.)** The antithesis of lawlessness is righteousness—*shalom* with Yehovah through covenantal loyalty ("*emunah.*") Sin, perversion, and rebellion sever this bond, as nothing impure can dwell in Yehovah's presence. **(See Habakkuk 1:13.)** Perfection demands death for sin. Not desiring even one of his created beings be destroyed, Yehovah bore upon himself the full weight of human lawlessness when he came as our Messiah and took on death in our stead. **(Isaiah 53:5–6; Romans 3:25.)** Yet, death could not conquer the Creator of life. Thus, Yeshua rose from *Sheol*, offering all who follow him to die and be born new, forever escaping death to take our place as sons and daughters of God. Our response to such merciful kindness is unwavering obedience—not powered by our own will, but empowered by the very Spirit of Yehovah who has inscribed his Torah on our renewed hearts **(See Jeremiah 31:31–34; Ezekiel 36:26–27)**, enabling his human family to walk in his ways. **(See Romans 8:4; Titus 2:11–14.)** Those who persist in *anomia* are sons of *Belial*, and will be unknown to the Messiah. **(Matthew 7:21–23)** Instead, the fruit of Yehovah's Spirit within man proves sonship **(See 1 John 3:4–10; Galatians 5:22-26; Matthew 13:36–43.)**

**Loyalty (*chesed* – God's part):** The Father's overwhelming and relentless pursuit of mankind to demonstrate kindness and covenantal loyalty (*ahavah*) is his mercy (*chesed*). It is in our Father's nature to part seas, erase guilt, and even humble himself to death in order to rescue his children. **(See Psalm 136; Exodus 34:6–7; Isaiah 53.)** **Loyalty (*emunah* – our part):** Our daily response to Yehovah's *chesed* is to loyally walk in his ways, submit ourselves to his will, and remain faithful to our Deliverer. The Hebrew *emunah* ("faithfulness; loyalty") derives from the root *aman*, meaning "to be firm, reliable, faithful," as in an unwavering trust that proves our allegiance through obedience. **(See Deuteronomy 30:15–20; Psalm 26:3.)** The covenantal dynamic is that Yehovah's *chesed* precedes and enables our *emunah*. We don't earn the Father's mercy—yet, its unfathomable magnitude humbles and draws humanity to respond with faithfulness. It's like a father who loves first, then guides and expects growth from his children. Thus, our relationship with Yehovah is like a father who desires what is best for his children. He offers them constant mercy, helps them grow, and expects them to follow the instructions that will safeguard them from danger. Loyalty is not a subjective, ideological agreement; rather, it is a daily choice to submit our will to that of our merciful Creator.

**Man (*Adam*):** *Adam* is more than just a first name. It means "mankind, humanity, or man." Derived from the word *adamah*, meaning "soil, ground, or earth," *adam* shares its root with *dam*, meaning "blood." Some Jewish mystics pursued further meaning by analyzing Hebrew language for potential allegories hidden within the letters that formed specific words. This sort of pictographic interpretation is purely speculative and not rooted in standard Hebrew lexicography. Reputable scholars seldom agree that this method is legitimate, as it can ignore etymology, be inconsistent and, at times, theologically dangerous. Some proponents argue, however, that the original definitions of some Ancient Hebrew words can be found within the actual letters that form the words, offering us a glimpse at that ancient meaning. Despite the probable illegitimacy of this approach, I have included it for demonstration purposes only. Some Jewish mystics utilized ancient pictographic scripts or symbols, similar in their use of imagery to Ancient Egyptian hieroglyphs, to propose some fascinating claims. Specifically, the word *adam*, formed by the Hebrew letters *Aleph, Dalet* and *Mem*, is claimed to contain a deeper understanding of the nature of this first man. In the proposition, the *Aleph*, being the first letter of the Hebrew alphabet, was represented by the ancient pictographic symbol of an ox head and meant "first" or "leader." Subsequently, the Ancient pictographic script of the *Dalet* was that of a doorway, meaning "door" or "path." Finally, the *Mem* was represented by a sharp, jagged wave shape that meant "chaos." Thus, some of these mystics have interpreted the word *adam*, ADM, as an allegory for the "first man who led humanity down the path of chaos." Despite the clear scholarly issues with this interpretive approach, at times it can present some interesting reflections. In this case, it can offer a contrast between the first Adam and the second Adam, the Messiah. The first man rebelled against Yehovah's commandment in the Garden and led humanity down the path of chaos. The Second Adam rejected the former's rebellion, restoring order through his own loyal obedience to Yehovah. Again, this is a subjective, secondary interpretation that should not be used as a primary, legitimate theological approach to Hebrew.

**Mercy:** See *Loyalty.*

**Messiah** (*Mashiach*): Anointed one, as in the one smeared, or covered, with oil symbolizing his selection by Yehovah to lead his people. (See Exodus 30:22–33; Psalm 133:2.) This figure was anointed to be a king or a priest, never both, except in the case of Yeshua *the* Messiah, who was Yehovah in flesh and whose reign would be as the eternal King *and* High Priest. (See Zechariah 6:9–15; Isaiah 9:6-7; 1 Samuel 8:7; Hebrews 1:3; Philippians 2:6–7; Colossians 2:9; Titus 2:13.) The term could also be applied to a prophet. (See Deuteronomy 18:15; Acts 3:22.) The Greek *Christos*, from which we get the English *Christ*, is not the last name of Yeshua. It is the title corresponding to the First Century view of *the Mashiach*. Through the Messiah, Yehovah would dwell upon the earth amongst his creation in the body of a man to demonstrate a life of perfect obedience, teaching us the intentions of God's Torah before ultimately bearing our sin when he died on our behalf. He did this in order to secure the eternal freedom of everyone who would call upon his name and follow after him, promising them protection from the death that was coming as the consequence of human rebellion and wickedness.

**Ministry** (*sharath*): To serve, to attend, as in to wait upon someone. (See Acts 3:26; Mark 10:35-45; John 13:12-20.) Yeshua was humble and gentle, doing only what he saw the Father do. (See Matthew 11:29; John 14:9; John 5:19.) We, too, are to serve one another in humility. (See Matthew 22:34-40; Matthew 25:31-46.) Ministry has nothing to do with building a name for ourselves, as the men in Babel sought to do. (See Genesis 11:4.) Instead, *sharath* is about humbly serving both God and our fellow man. (See Genesis 12:2.) If we joyfully serve one another with compassion, generosity and kindness, our Father will provide for all our needs. (See Matthew 6:25-33; Philippians 4:10-20.)

**The New Testament** (*Brit HaChadashah*): Collection of twenty-seven documents, including: 1) four accounts of the Messiah's genealogy, birth, teachings, miracles, testing, arrest, trial, death, and resurrection, along with key figures and life in Judea; 2) a record of the immediate aftermath of his resurrection, the arrival of Yehovah's Spirit, and the rapid spread of God's Kingdom to the Gentiles; 3) a series of letters by early apostles to guide those who trusted in Yeshua; and 4) a prophetic vision. Written fifteen to sixty-five years after the resurrection, these documents were first named in a single list around AD 180. Together, they proclaim the fulfillment of the promised New Covenant.(See Isaiah 55:3–5; Isaiah 59:20–21; Isaiah 61:1–3, 8–9; Hosea 2:18–20; Jeremiah 31:31–34; Ezekiel 36:24–28; Ezekiel 37:24–28; Malachi 3:1–4.)

**Obey** (*shama*): To listen and obey; to hear, as in "to take to heart." *Shama* is not an auditory function, as in one's physical sense of hearing. Rather, it is to do what has been heard. (See James 1:22.)

**One** (*echad*): See *Echad.*

**The Old Testament** (*Tanakh*): There are various disputes within Christianity, as well as between some Christian traditions and Judaism, as to the list of scrolls or writings that make up the Old Testament, though the list of books found within Protestant Christianity and Orthodox Judaism are identical, though in a slightly different order. Yet, the term "Old Testament" is largely relegated to Christianity and not Judaism. The term refers to a set of scrolls containing various instructions, prophecies and other writings that, together, make up the divinely inspired words of Yehovah, the God of Abraham, Isaac, and Jacob, as transmitted through various men, and which existed prior to the arrival of the Messiah. To some, the term "old" can denote something outdated, as in replaced by something "new." And though there is certainly a New Covenant, the Tanakh contains far more than simply the former covenant. *Tanakh* is simply an acronym used for Torah, Nevi'im, and Ketuvim, wherein the Torah (instruction) is the five books of Moses, the Nevi'im are the prophets and the Ketuvim are the other writings, such as Job, Psalms, Proverbs, etc. Thus, the Tanakh holds a profoundly irreplaceable importance for the followers of Yeshua. (See 2 Timothy 3:16.) Note that at the time of writing of the aforementioned passage, the "New Testament" had yet to be completed or compiled. For New Testament authors, the term "scripture" was widely accepted to mean the content exclusively found within the *Tanakh*.

**Passover** (*Pesach*): Proper name for the first biblical Feast Day observed each year. The day served as a reminder of Yehovah's deliverance of Israel when he stood over the homes of the people who had placed the blood of a perfect lamb over their doorway, protecting them from death. The blood served as a pledge of allegiance to the Creator. (See Exodus 12:13; 1 Peter 1:19; 1 Corinthians 5:7.) The Messiah died on Passover, and his blood marks those loyal to him, protecting them from death and offering them eternal life by writing their names in the (Lamb's) Book of Life. (See Matthew 26:2; Revelation 21:27; Revelation 20:15; Exodus 32:30-33; Daniel 12:1-3; Revelation 13:8.) The traditional definition of the term *pesach* is simply "to pass over." Recent scholarship, however, may offer insight into a different understanding of the word. Specifically, Targum Onkelos and Targum Pseudo-Jonathan, suggest that the term means, "to spare" or "to protect," as reflected in the Aramaic word *chamas* used in Targum Onkelos for *pesach* in Exodus 12:13, implying protection or sparing from harm. The Qal perfect third-person masculine singular verb form of the root *pasach* in Isaiah 31:5 describes God "protecting" or "shielding" Jerusalem as hovering birds, where "to spare" is a more precise English rendering than "to pass over," as it emphasizes active, divine safeguarding. The term is encapsulated by the anthropomorphic imagery of the Creator using his right hand both to destroy his enemies and simultaneously protect his people. (See Exodus 6:6; Exodus 15:6; Psalm 20:6; Psalm 138:7.)

*Rabbi* (teacher): Teacher or master, as in an expert schoolmaster; regarded as an authority in regards to religious practice. Traditionally, a rabbi would select students to spend a period of time following him in order to perpetuate learning from one generation to the next. Yeshua was a Jewish rabbi and had twelve Jewish students, most of which were likely younger than he, during his years of ministry. In Jewish discipleship, the best student spoke only what he heard from his rabbi and so mirrored him that if you've seen the disciple, you've seen the rabbi—a standard Yeshua fulfilled perfectly. (See John 8:28; John 10:30; John 14:9-10.) The formal rabbinic ordination system (*semikhah*) seen later in the Talmud was still developing in Jesus' time; thus, he didn't attend a rabbinic academy like Hillel or Shammai's, but functioned as an independent rabbi with divine authority. (See Mark 11:28-33.)

**Rebellion** (*pesha*): To break away (from a just authority); to rebel, revolt, or transgress. The idea is that of a willful breaking away from or betrayal of a relationship. Another word for rebel in Hebrew is *marah*. Where *pesha* refers to a willful betrayal of a relationship by stepping outside the agreed upon parameters, *marah* describes the general state of defiance, which is often born out of bitterness, anger, or animosity. Idolatry, witchcraft, stubbornness, and unbelief were some of the actions viewed as rebellion. Rebellion against Yehovah is a breach of covenantal agreement, often involving a conscious rejection of His authority. Such rebellion disrupts the relationship and may incur divine judgment.

**Reconcile** (*kaphar*): To cover over; atone. When Yehovah decided to blot out all of creation except for Noah, his wife, his sons, and his sons' wives for the widespread wickedness, rebellion and abominations taking place within mankind, he instructed Noah to use something called "pitch" in order to seal up the Ark on the inside and outside, making it watertight. This substance protected the ark from the destruction of Yehovah's judgement. The pitch (*koper*) used to cover the ark comes from the same root as atonement (*kapar*), both meaning 'to cover.' In the same way, Yehovah covers his people with the blood of the Lamb, protecting us from the judgment that destroys the enemies of God. In both cases, the covering, or reconciliation, was a merciful provision offered by the Creator, but one that required application.

**Redeem (*ga'al*):** To redeem or buy back (a person, inheritance, or freedom), often by a kinsman-redeemer (*go'el*); to ransom; to deliver by power; to avenge bloodshed. First used in Exodus 6:6 for Yehovah's redemption of Israel from Egypt through judgment. In human law, it includes restoring lost property or status; in divine usage, it emphasizes liberation and covenant restoration, with full restitution more fully expressed in prophetic promises.

**Repent (*shuv*):** To turn (back); to return; to restore. Unlike the Latin *paenitēre* and its English form "repent," *shuv* does not mean to feel regret or to say sorry. In fact, it is neither a feeling nor an apology. *Shuv* is the abrupt change of course, abandoning once defiant and rebellious behaviors that put the person at odds with the Creator in the first place. Turning back to God's Torah leads to life and peace. (**See Ezekiel 18:21-32.**) Note that the Torah spells out the required restitution when one sins against his neighbor. Simply apologizing to God is not sufficient. In Luke's account of Zacchaeus, the tax collector's fourfold repayment exceeds the standard penalty for most thefts found in the Torah, which was typically double or principal plus one-fifth, and likely draws from the maximum penalty in **Exodus 22:1** for a sheep that's sold or slaughtered, instead of the lighter double penalty of **Exodus 22:4**. By choosing fourfold restitution, Zacchaeus goes *beyond* the standard requirement for fraud or extortion and aligns with the Torah's most severe theft penalty. By choosing the harshest restitution, Zacchaeus demonstrated his desire to fully right his wrongs. Yeshua covers our transgressions against Yehovah, but we must right the wrongs we've committed against one another. (**See Luke 19:1-10; Matthew 5:23-24.**)

**Righteous (*tsaddiq*):** A person who is just, upright, and faithful, living at peace with God's Torah and covenant. One who is *tsaddiq* exhibits Torah-observant behavior, ethical integrity, compassion, and justice, maintaining good standing with the Creator through faithfulness, atonement, and continual alignment to the will of Yehovah. In contrast to the wicked, the *tsaddiq* upholds God's standards, defends the oppressed, and trusts in His promises, as seen in figures like Noah and Abraham. The *tsaddiq* is not perfect, but gets back up when he falls. (**See Proverbs 24:16.**)

**Sabbath/Shabbat:** From Hebrew verb shabath, meaning "cease/rest", the seventh day is sanctified in Genesis by Yehovah and instructed in the Fourth Commandment. Unlike the modern counting of time wherein the new day begins at midnight, with its Egyptian, Mesopotamian, and medieval roots, biblical time reckons days from sundown to sundown. Thus, Yeshua observed Sabbath from Friday at sunset through Saturday at sunset. No biblical text authorizes any transition to another day. Addressing common arguments for Sunday: The "Lord's Day" (**see Rev 1:10**) is undefined, while Old Testament precedent links "Yehovah's holy day" to Sabbath (**See Isaiah 58:13-14.**) The occurrence in **Acts 20:7** simply refers to a single event that began on a Saturday after sunset. Paul's speech went until midnight, thus the "first day of the week" here was a Saturday night, not a Sunday. **First Corinthians 16:2** orders the Corinthians to put money aside once a month to help those in Jerusalem facing famine—it is not a shift in Sabbath. **Romans 14:5** is concerning fast days, not the Sabbath. Lastly, Constantine's AD 321 edict was civil, blending Dies Sol worship; later ecclesiastical claims (e.g., Catholic) lack an apostolic precedent and violate the Decalogue's permanence. The New Testament lacks even one Sabbath debate, unlike circumcision requirements, implying its unrivaled continuity. If Yehovah wanted it changed, we would expect the Messiah to mention it, yet Sunday worship only emerges post-AD 70. In **Colossians 2:16-17**, Paul tells the Gentile community not to be condemned by Ascetics with their practices of extreme self-deprivation who had been mocking them for resting on Sabbath and enjoying feast days, since those appointed times were meant to foreshadow what was to come. In **1 Corinthians 7:17–19**, Paul emphasizes upholding the commandments as a rule to all churches. He never excludes the Sabbath. Supporters of a shift to Sunday suggest it occurred in the early church as a way to honor the resurrection of Christ, though no New Testament text supports this claim. The Messiah kept Sabbath unchanged, upheld all the commandments, and affirmed their permanence. (**See Matt 5:17–19.**) Furthermore, the precise timing of the resurrection is unknown, as the tomb was empty before the first visitor arrived on Sunday at dawn (**See John 20:1**); thus, the Messiah could have risen anytime after the end of Sabbath, with over five hours left until midnight in Jerusalem during that time of year. In this way, Saturday evening is as valid a claim for a resurrection as Sunday morning. Either way, honoring the resurrection each week is certainly not problematic on its own, so long as the Sabbath remains the Sabbath. On it, everyone in God's family has been invited to rest, knowing that Yehovah, not us, is in control. There is much more that could be said, but not within the limitations of this book.

**Salvation (*Yeshua*):** A proper noun, as in a name, being the diminutive of *Yehoshua*. The proper noun is also a theophoric name—in this case, created by combining two other words. Those words are *Yeho*, the shortened form of the divine name, *Yehovah*, and *shua*, a derivative of its root *yasha*, which means "to save," "to deliver," "to rescue," or "to bring to safety." Thus, *Yeshua* literally means, "Yehovah is salvation," or "Yehovah's deliverer." Unlike the men who came before him, *Yeshua* would be an eternal deliverer, a great high priest and immortal king, bringing humanity into the promised land of eternal life.

**Sons of God (*bene ha Elohim*):** Created spiritual beings that are part of Yehovah's Divine Council, having been given roles in the governance of the world, though some were cast down for their involvement in rebellion. An additional usage is that of a title given to human beings who, despite their natural weaknesses, have joined Yehovah's family via the Messiah's redemption and their loyal obedience. (**See Ecclesiastes 12:7; Hosea 1:10; Luke 20:36; John 1:12; John 11:51-52; Romans 8:14-17; Romans 9:26; 1 Corinthians 6:3; 1 Corinthians 15:42–49; 2 Corinthians 5:1–5; Galatians 4:4-7; Ephesians 2:1-22; Philippians 2:15; Hebrews 2:5-8; Hebrews 2:10-11; 1 John 3:1-10; Revelation 2:26-27; Revelation 3:21; Revelation 20:4-6; Revelation 22:5**) The theory proposes that some of the powerful spiritual beings who once held the title "Sons of God" and were created without the limitations of human weakness, rebelled and were cast down. (**See Genesis 6; Deuteronomy 32:8-9; Job 1-2; Psalm 82; Isaiah 14:12; 2 Peter 2:4**) Now, the Body of Messiah, made up of human beings who have been redeemed and chosen loyal obedience to Yehovah are (and will fully be in the future) glorified, and given the title once held by those fallen spiritual rebels. For more information, check out, *The Unseen Realm* by Dr. Michael S. Heiser.

**Sin (*chata*):** To miss; to go wrong; to incur guilt; lawlessness, according to **1 John 3:4**, wherein lawlessness (*anomia*) is not observing Yehovah's Torah, or law. Straying outside Yehovah's established boundary takes us outside his protection and blessing, into a place where death and destruction exist. Laws exist in society as a threshold for what is allowed. They are not meant to be arbitrary, but have preservation in mind. Likewise, the Torah provides us with Yehovah's commandments that exist to protect us from pain and death. The commandments are more than just rules, they are God's teachings. In fact, the word "teach" or *yarah*, means "to shoot," as in an arrow. In the Ancient Near East, fathers taught their sons how to shoot so that they could protect themselves and their families, as well as provide food. God's Torah is his teaching for our instruction, so that we are protected from death and have access to the blessing of God's provision. Sin, on the other hand, is like shooting an arrow and missing the target. (**See Ezekiel 18:21-24.**) (**See also Matthew 7:23; Matthew 13:41; Matthew 23:28; Matthew 24:12; Romans 6:19; 2 Corinthians 6:14; 1 Timothy 1:9; Titus 2:14; Hebrews 1:9; 1 John 3:4.**)

**Shalom (*peace*):** Far more than absence of war, shalom is the covenantal wholeness of people, land, and creation under Yehovah's reign. It flows from obedience to the Creator, active justice (*mishpat*), and righteousness (*tzedakah*), and manifests in practical, spiritual and emotional ways, such as joy, assurance, contentment, prosperity, safety, fertility, and overall social harmony. *Shalom* is both a present blessing for the loyal and an eschatological hope—fully realized when the Messiah returns to establish everlasting *shalom*. (**See Isaiah 9:1–7; Ezekiel 34:25-31; Numbers 6:22–27.**) In Yeshua the Messiah, *shalom* is offered as reconciliation with Yehovah.

**Shavuot** (*Pentecost*): Literally, "weeks" in Hebrew and "fiftieth" in Greek, is the festival that arrives exactly fifty days after the *Firstfruits* offering on 16 Nisan. In the Torah, counting begins the day after the Passover Sabbath, when the priest waves the first sheaf of barley before Yehovah, marking the start of the grain harvest. (**See Leviticus 23:10–11, 15–16.**) Tradition links Shavuot the completion of this count—on 6 Sivan—to the giving of the Ten Commandments at Mount Sinai, which occurred approximately fifty days after Israel's exodus from Egypt. The New Testament presents a precise fulfillment of the same calendar. Yeshua is crucified on Passover (14 Nisan) as the ultimate Passover lamb. He rests in the tomb on the festival Sabbath (15 Nisan), then rises following Sabbath—the very day the wave sheaf is offered, becoming "the firstfruits of those who have fallen asleep." (**See 1 Corinthians 15:20.**) Exactly fifty days later on Shavuot, the Spirit of Yehovah descended upon Yeshua's followers who were gathered in a house on or near Mount Zion—most likely a roofed chamber or portico attached to the Temple complex, where pilgrims gathered for the morning sacrifice and prayer. The sound drew multitudes from the Temple courts (Acts 2:1–6), and three thousand were immersed in the nearby mikvehs that same day. Whereas the Torah had been inscribed on tablets of stone at Sinai in the former covenant, the Spirit of Yehovah now writes the Torah on human hearts, fulfilling the promise of a New Covenant. (**See Jeremiah 31:31–34; Ezekiel 36:26–27.**) At Sinai, covenant unfaithfulness brought death to three thousand; on this *Shavuot*, covenant faithfulness brought eternal life to three thousand. Thus, the spring feasts (*Pesach*, Firstfruits, and *Shavuot*) find their full meaning in the death and resurrection of Messiah, and outpouring of Yehovah's Spirit.

**Steal** (*ganav*): To secretly or deceptively take, or carry away, what rightfully belongs to another; to kidnap. In the latter sense, kidnapping involves taking and enslaving a life created by Yehovah against its will. The punishment for such wickedness is death. (**See Exodus 21:16.**)

**Teach** (*yarah*): To throw; to shoot; to cast (as an arrow); to point out or direct (a path). The Hebrew root *yrh*, is conceptually linked to the Ugaritic *yry*, meaning "to shoot," but comes directly from the Akkadian *waru*, meaning "to direct." The two Proto-Semitic words, though unique, share an underlying connection with regard to guidance. Thus, *yarah* is linked to both direction and shooting, as in guiding an arrow to a target. (**See Leviticus 10:11.**) In fact, the participle, *yoreh*, means "an archer" or "one who shoots." *Yoreh* also specifically refers to the "early rain" that falls in the autumn, providing essential moisture to guide the seed into growth. (**See Deuteronomy 11:14.**) In the Ancient Hebraic mind, parents and teachers were to instruct their children, sending them along the path to life. Though *Torah*, meaning "instruction" or "direction," comes from the parallel root meaning "to point out, to instruct," *yarah* and *torah* converge in biblical thought, wherein an archer shoots toward the mark (*yarah*), and the parent offers instruction (*torah*) for the path of life.

**Torah: See Law.**

**Trust: See Belief.**

**Truth** (*emet*): The term signifies a deep truth, yet something beyond mere factually precise information. Derived from the root verb *aman*, meaning to support, make firm, or be trustworthy. In Hebrew, *emet* is written using the first (*aleph*), middle (*mem*), and last (*tov*) letters of the Hebrew alphabet. Thus, sages and rabbis have often taught that *emet* encompasses all things and cannot exist without context. Furthermore, *emet* goes beyond the intellectual, theoretical, or conceptual world, to include practical realities. For instance, *emet* is not simply an accurate ideology. It requires a fuller demonstration of that reality in the life of the one who knows them to be true. In other words, *emet* is rooted in a truthful way of living, wherein one's conduct aligns perfectly with what they say they believe to be true. In this way, *emet* is an enduring concept found in the nature of Yehovah and within the world that he has created, presenting something that is complete and good, lacking nothing.

**Turn: See Repent.**

**Wickedness** (*resha'*): Though the term denotes moral guilt or wrongdoing, *resha'* is portrayed as wickedness, unjust, and morally-corrupted actions, marking a deliberate departure from Yehovah's path. In other words, it is a willful and defiant turning away from Yehovah's ways, which were given to protect humanity from ruin, suffering, and destruction. A person living in *resha'* is not merely erring but embracing a self-willed path. Yet, the offender can find restoration, as forgiveness is extended to those who return to Yehovah's path, trust in the redemption offered by the Messiah, and walk in loyal obedience.

**Worship** (*shachah* or *avodah*): *Shachah* corresponds most accurately to the Greek New Testament word *proskyneō*, meaning "to bow down" or "to worship." *Avodah*, on the other hand, corresponds most closely to the Greek words *latreia* or *latreuō*, meaning "service" or "worship." The two Hebrew terms express different facets of what the English word "worship" encompasses, overlapping in concept but not in meaning. Depending on how the author uses the English term, worship may refer to bowing down in reverence—submitting oneself in humility as a physical demonstration of loyalty—or to the work or service of worship (see entry on Ministry). (**See Matthew 15:1–9; Isaiah 29:13–14.**) Scripture teaches that true worship is not found merely in sacrifices, but in an obedient lifestyle that imitates the character and nature of Yehovah. (**See Isaiah 58; 1 Samuel 15:22–23.**)

**Yehovah** (*Yahweh*): Transliteration of the Hebrew Tetragrammaton—the four-letter divine Name (YHWH) first appearing in Genesis 2:4. The original pronunciation of the Name is uncertain, as the text preserves only consonants, and no universally accepted vocalization exists. In this book, I use the form "Yehovah," following the work of Dr. Nehemia Gordon, who argues for this pronunciation on the basis of over 1,000 Hebrew manuscripts that vocalize the Name with the vowels *Sheva*, *Cholam*, and *Kamatz*, and linguistic evidence suggesting the ancient pronunciation of the letter *Vav* was "v" rather than "w." Gordon further proposes that "Yehovah" reflects God's eternal nature, connecting the Name to the Hebrew verbs meaning "was," "is," and "will be," though many scholars view this as unlikely. Critics maintain that the Masoretic vowel points attached to YHWH reflect scribal conventions—specifically the practice of placing the vowels of *Adonai* onto the divine Name—rather than the original pronunciation. Gordon contends that these vowel points instead preserve the authentic vocalization. Regardless of the pronunciation debate, it is important to note the relationship between Yehovah and the divine self-identification of Exodus 3:14, wherein the Creator says, *Ehyeh Asher Ehyeh* ("I Am Who I Am.") *Ehyeh* is the first-person form of the verb *hayah* ("to be"), while Yehovah is commonly understood as a third-person form, or derivative expressing "He is/was/will be." Though the exact grammatical relationship is debated, the two expressions are thematically and theologically connected: *Ehyeh* reveals the Creator's existence from his perspective, while Yehovah expresses the reality from the perspective of His people.

**Yeshua: See Salvation.**

# Scripture References

**Genesis:**
1:26-27; 2:4-8; 2:15; 2:24; 3:1-24; 3:19; 4:1-7; 4:12; 6:1-8; 11:4; 12:1-3; 12:2; 15:1-21; 17:1-27

**Exodus:**
3:14; 6:5-6; 12:1-51; 12:12-13; 15:6; 19:6; 20:3-9; 21:10; 21:16; 22:1; 22:4; 30:22-33; 32:30-33; 34:6-7

**Leviticus:**
6:1-7; 10:11; 19:15; 19:35-36; 20:10; 23:10-11; 23:15-16; 25:35-37

**Numbers:**
6:22-27; 32:15

**Deuteronomy:**
6:4-9; 11:14; 12:8; 13:4; 13:13; 18:13; 18:15; 19:16-19; 22:25-27; 24:14-15; 25:5; 30:6; 30:15-20; 32:4; 32:8-9

**1 Samuel:**
2:12; 8:7; 15:22-23

**1 Kings:**
8:27; 14:8

**Job:**
1:1-2:13

**Psalms:**
2:7-8; 19:7; 20:6; 26:3; 31:5; 32:1; 40:6-8; 82:1-8; 82:8; 89:14; 98:2-3; 127:3-5; 133:2; 136:1-26; 138:7; 139:23-24

**Proverbs:**
1:8-19; 5:1-23; 6:12; 6:16-19; 10:9; 19:17; 21:13; 22:1; 24:16

**Ecclesiastes:**
12:7

**Isaiah:**
1:11-17; 9:1-7; 9:6-7; 14:12-17; 29:13-14; 30:18; 45:22; 49:6; 53:1-12; 53:5-6; 55:3-5; 55:6-9; 56:6-8; 57:15; 58:6-10; 58:13-14; 59:20-21; 61:1-3; 61:8-9; 66:1-2

**Jeremiah:**
23:23-24; 31:31-34

**Ezekiel:**
18:21-32; 20:39; 28:17; 34:25-31; 36:24-28; 36:27; 37:24-28

**Daniel:**
12:1-3

**Hosea:**
1:10; 2:18-20; 6:6

**Micah:**
6:6-8

**Habakkuk:**
1:13

**Malachi:**
3:1-4

**Matthew:**
5:9; 5:17-20; 5:21-26; 5:23-24; 5:27-32; 5:33-37; 5:43-48; 5:48; 6:25-33; 7:12; 7:15-20; 7:21-23; 11:29; 12:9-12; 13:36-43; 13:41; 15:1-9; 16:24; 18:21-35; 19:18; 20:20-28; 22:34-40; 23:28; 24:12; 25:31-46; 26:2; 26:28; 26:59-61

**Mark:**
7:1-13; 10:35-45; 11:28-33; 14:55-59

**Luke:**
6:27-36; 14:27-33; 19:1-10; 20:36

**John:**
1:1-4; 1:12-13; 1:29; 3:16-21; 5:19; 8:28; 10:10; 10:30; 11:49-53; 13:1-17; 13:12-20; 14:8-11; 14:9-10; 14:15-24; 14:23; 16:33; 17:21; 20:1

**Acts:**
2:1-6; 3:22; 3:26; 6:11-14; 10:1-4; 20:7

**Romans:**
3:21-31; 3:25; 5:10-11; 6:15-18; 6:19; 8:2; 8:4; 8:14-17; 8:14-23; 9:26; 11:1-32; 12:1-21

**1 Corinthians:**
2:10-13; 3:16-17; 5:7; 6:3; 6:9-11; 6:19-20; 7:17-19; 13:1-13; 15:20; 15:42-49; 16:2

**2 Corinthians:**
3:3; 5:1-5; 5:20; 6:14-18; 10:3-5

**Galatians:**
2:20; 3:26; 4:4-7; 5:16-25; 5:22-26

**Ephesians:**
1:7; 2:1-22; 2:8-10; 2:11-22; 2:21-22

**Philippians:**
2:6-7; 2:15; 4:8-9; 4:10-20

**Colossians:**
2:9; 2:16; 2:16-17

**1 Timothy:**
1:9; 6:17-18

**2 Timothy:**
3:16

**Titus:**
2:11-14; 2:13

**Hebrews:**
1:3; 1:9; 2:5-8; 2:10-11; 7:11-28; 9:11-28; 9:14; 10:1-31

**James:**
1:22; 2:14-26; 2:15-16; 4:17

**1 Peter:**
1:19; 2:9

**2 Peter:**
2:4

**1 John:**
1:7; 3:1-2; 3:4; 3:17-18; 3:21-22; 5:2-3

**Jude:**
1:6-7

**Revelation:**
1:5-6; 2:26-27; 3:17-21; 3:21; 5:6; 7:9; 13:8; 20:4-6; 20:15; 21:8; 21:27; 22:5; 22:15

## About the Author

Daniel Owen is an author and award-winning documentary photojournalist whose work has been featured in publications around the globe. He has been a contributing speaker for the U.S. Holocaust Memorial Museum's "Voices on Antisemitism" series following his work documenting Auschwitz survivors in Romania. His work focuses on subcultures, religion and traditional practices. He has collaborated with newspapers throughout the U.S. covering subjects ranging from U.S. presidential elections to python hunters in the Everglades, and has been embedded in long term projects covering everything from America's drug epidemic to Gypsies in Transylvania. He also served as the Director of Photography at the Los Alamos National Laboratory before relocating to Eastern Europe with his wife and children.

Owen is not a Biblical scholar, he is a journalist. His approach to theology, therefore, is rooted in the journalistic process wherein ideological preferences are set aside and tested against then evidence of original source materials, and Biblical texts are examined in light of their Ancient Near Eastern context. To that end, he has spent nearly twenty years earning an informal education in the history, language, culture and mythology found in and around the texts of the Bible. In his work, Owen seeks to deconstruct the lenses Christians often unknowingly use to filter the Bible through their traditions. His goal is to encourage believers to see the Bible as its authors intended and, in doing so, know who God is and what he expects of each of us.

*For more information, please visit:*
www.danielowenphoto.com